Praise for *Simplify Your Life*

Simplify Your Life: Get Organized and Stay That Way! is full of wonderful tips and systems. Marcia has a special flair for teaching in a very simple, digestible, and manageable manner. Very useful!

JULIE MORGENSTERN
AMERICA'S #1 ORGANIZING EXPERT
AUTHOR OF *TIME MANAGEMENT FROM THE INSIDE OUT*

Simplify Your Life: Get Organized and Stay That Way! teaches lifelong habits for women committed to personal excellence and success in life. A life well lived includes organizing and managing all the "pieces" to positively influence those around them. Highly practical! I recommend it.

DR. DENIS WAITLEY
WORLD-RENOWNED KEYNOTE SPEAKER AND PRODUCTIVITY CONSULTANT
AUTHOR OF *SEEDS OF GREATNESS*

Marcia offers inspiration and innovative ways of looking at age-old problems faced by busy women everywhere. A "must read" if you have big dreams and limited time.

BARBARA HEMPHILL
PAST PRESIDENT
NATIONAL ASSOCIATION OF PROFESSIONAL ORGANIZERS
AUTHOR OF *TAMING THE PAPER TIGER*

Simplify
your life

GET ORGANIZED AND
STAY THAT WAY!

MARCIA RAMSLAND

THOMAS NELSON
Since 1798

NASHVILLE   DALLAS   MEXICO CITY   RIO DE JANEIRO

Published in Nashville, Tennessee by Thomas Nelson. Thomas Nelson is a registered trademark of Thomas Nelson, Inc.

Thomas Nelson, Inc. titles may be purchased in bulk for educational, business, fund-raising, or sales promotional use. For information, please e-mail SpecialMarkets@ThomasNelson.com.

Scripture quotations are from the HOLY BIBLE: NEW INTERNATIONAL VERSION. © 1973, 1978, 1984 by International Bible Society. Used by permission of Zondervan Publishing House. All rights reserved.

The names and identities of clients mentioned have been changed or concealed in composites to protect their privacy. For those who granted permission to do so, their names and details about their lives appear as they happened.

Library of Congress Cataloging-in-Publication Data

Ramsland, Marcia.
   Simplify your life : get organized and stay that way / By Marcia Ramsland.
     p. cm.
   ISBN: 978-0-8499-4442-0 (softcover)
   1. Home economics. 2. Time management. I. Title.
TX147.R36 2003
640—dc22   2003017824

Printed in the United States of America
10 11 12 13 EPAC 19 18 17 16

This book is dedicated to . . .

all women (and those who live with them)
in search of a simpler, more satisfying life,

my clients and audiences who shaped
my thinking by their passionate quests to get organized,

and to you, my new friend,
as we walk side by side to simplify *your* life.

CONTENTS

Foreword

I absolutely love order. While not admitting to being a control freak, my preference in life is to run on time, stay fairly organized, accomplish my goals, and keep stuff tidy. When I do, I'm free to enjoy life and the people I love.

The problem? There's never enough time.

That's why I loved Marcia Ramsland the first time I met her. She had such fun, simple, and practical ideas to help make life less complicated. Sitting through a seminar with her gave me a very hopeful feeling that help was on the way. She demonstrated that by making a few simple changes in daily routines, life could be more organized and a lot tidier.

Simplify Your Life is like your own personal management trainer. With heartfelt encouragement and warmth, Marcia helps us find easy, clever ways of staying organized. Best of all, she doesn't lose sight of God's design and how He's always working within us, nurturing growth and necessary change. He's a God of order, the One who gave creative order to the universe, and He desires order in our lives. A "Simple Prayer" at the end of each chapter is our gentle reminder of His power and grace to do for us what we cannot do for ourselves.

Life may not be simple, but it can certainly be simplified.

Mary Graham
President
Women of Faith

Introduction

Flash back to twenty years ago: Late one afternoon after another ordinary but frustrating day, I was cooking spaghetti and becoming increasingly annoyed with each stir of the tomato sauce. My preschool daughters, Christy and Lisa, were slowly emptying the dishes out of the dishwasher and cluttering up the counters while my six-month-old son, Mark, hovered around my ankles. I was trying hard to be productive and get things done, but it seemed that everything I had done lately—even preparing a simple meal—was being sabotaged. I felt as if I had no accomplishments to show for the past three hours (or the past three days, for that matter).

Soon I realized that the spaghetti noodles weren't the only things about to boil over in my crowded kitchen. The pressure inside of me had been mounting all day. As I furiously chopped the onions to make up for lost time, I suddenly exploded, "My *life* is worth more than this!"

Christy and Lisa stopped and looked up at me, unable to comprehend my outburst. Mark stopped crawling around. I gasped at the words that had erupted from my mouth as I pulled the boiling spaghetti noodles off the stove.

My life is worth more than this? I slowly pondered what I had just said. Did I mean my life was worth more than raising children? Surely not. Did I mean I was above cooking meals, washing dishes, making beds, cleaning up messes, going grocery shopping, and constantly being interrupted?

Well, not exactly, but being on call around the clock was getting old real fast.

"Don't worry," I said as I calmed the little ones. "Everything's going to be okay." Reassuring the children failed to reassure *me*, however. That's when I realized that I was waking up every morning feeling exhausted, and frustration was becoming a regular part of my everyday life.

This was not a life—running myself ragged from morning till night and feeling as if I had accomplished very little by day's end. Every time I looked around and saw cluttered counters, mail piling up, bills to be paid, letters to be answered, laundry baskets full of clothes to be folded, I felt like screaming, "Why can't I get anything done?!"

On that memorable evening in my kitchen, I realized that more disarray would indeed be heading my way . . . unless someone in my family could get it together. And judging by the ages of everyone in the kitchen, I realized that it had to be me.

That was the moment I decided to change.

Organize My Life, Please

Over the next several weeks, I earnestly prayed for help to get organized. I read all I could find on the subject, only to find everything was written by logical, left-brained men for the workplace. The typical organizing advice consisted of these marching orders:

1. Make a list.
2. Start at the top.
3. Check things off until you are finished.

That wasn't the world I was living in. My answer to Mr. Organized and his spotless desk was similar to what most women feel when they are being told what to do: "Even if I could find the list, I wouldn't feel like doing a list!"

I had tried my hand at making lists, but they just weren't working for me. Wasn't there a better way? I wasn't looking for a new method to organize my closets or tips to organize my spices. I was looking for something more—a way to organize my life.

If necessity is the mother of invention, then I should have some answers fast. I began by scrutinizing my problem areas. These fell under four categories:

- Time issues and related paper piles
- Home itself
- Special projects beyond the routine
- General daily frustrations

After much research and many dead ends, I ended up creating systems that worked. In my excitement I started teaching organizing principles back in 1985. I also discovered I was part of an emerging group of entrepreneurs called professional organizers—people who create practical solutions for complicated situations. We were discovering a rising need for answers in dealing with busy lifestyles.

The need and demand from the public for answers snowballed from that point on, and I began teaching seminars, appearing on radio and television shows, and sharing tips in national magazines. After working with clients for all those years in professional settings from Rochester, New York, to San Diego, California, I felt led to share my organizing message with those who need the skills just as much: busy women wanting to simplify their complicated lives.

I have written *Simplify Your Life: Get Organized and Stay That Way!* to support the myriad of challenges in managing a home, a family, a career, and community activities. I believe that when we organize and simplify our lives, we move away from busyness and crisis into order and freedom. It is a satisfying way to live.

Let Me Be Your Chauffeur

Many organizing books are like a map—they tell us what to do and how to get there. But I've found that most women want a chauffeur, someone to keep them company as they drive to a new destination.

Allow me to be that chauffeur. I will help you navigate the tricky detours of simplifying life in the midst of your already busy schedule. We will wind our way through client stories, practical systems and tips, and times of personal reflection to get you on your way. And I've even included a sample prayer at the end of each chapter since I've found that most lasting changes take strength from inside and outside myself.

The book is set up in three sections, covering your time and paperwork, your everyday systems at home, and special seasons of your life. The book progressively picks up speed as it goes along, so be sure to make it all the way through. At the end I promise I will even walk you through transitions, those rare but difficult times in life when everything you put together seems to fall apart.

My message is about living life well. And if you've ever wondered, "Can my life get any better than this?" the answer is a resounding "Yes!" You may just need a fresh vision. Let's have some fun and simplify life together for good—for your good and the good of those around you.

—Marcia Ramsland
Professional Organizer

one

Simplifying Is a Personal Journey

Most people spend more time planning their vacation, a remodeling project, or their wedding than they spend planning their lives.

—Dr. Denis Waitley
author and motivational speaker

Ah, I hear the sound of waves gently rolling onto the shore. The sun warms my face, and my toes wiggle in the sand. For now my novel lies on my lap. And all I have to do is occupy myself until dinner is served. I can do whatever I want. I am living the simplified life . . . I'm on vacation.

Is vacation the only place to enjoy a simplified life? Yes and no. To simplify life the rest of the year is to create that same vacation feeling—relaxation, enjoyment, and ease.

But not every vacation turns out to be that relaxing, as you know. It takes dreaming, planning, and action. And so does simplifying your life.

Simplifying your life is a journey you choose to take. To do things you enjoy, you must find the time to do them. To make your life easier, you must find better ways of doing things. To spend time with people you value, you must say good-bye to a jam-packed schedule.

Simplified living includes everything about you and welcomes your personal style of getting things done. Like a vacation, this journey is shaped by who you are and what you like to do. It recognizes personal habits you practice, such as how much time it takes to get dressed in the morning, when you read the mail, and if and how you relax in the evenings. It is all about you and what you do every day.

Can You Simplify Your Life?

There are two very good questions to ask yourself if you want to simplify your life any more than it is. The first one is this: "How much of my life do I actually control?" If you recognize what you can control, you have opportunities to modify it for a better life.

The second question to ask is, "Am I willing to make any changes in my life?" Put quite simply, if you are willing to change, you can. If you don't want to change, you won't. It's all up to you.

Where Are We Going?

This book is meant to help you on your journey of life. Instead of being a how-to resource pointing you toward your destination, it is a journey with a chauffeur to keep you company on the way. As your chauffeur, I will drive you from complex to simple, from busy to calm. As a professional organizer who learned things the hard way before developing a track record of helping thousands of clients and audience participants across the country, I will share tips on how to do things differently. (And if you missed my story in the introduction, you might be interested in reading it now.)

Any day is a great day to begin simplifying your life. Let's get started.

A Desire to Conquer the World

One summer when my three children were home from school, I determined to simplify my life by getting the house back into shape. With great resolve, I wrote a detailed to-do list that would conquer the world—or at least every basket of laundry, home improvement project, and cluttered nook and cranny in the house. Then the phone rang. My neighbor was on the line. "We're going over to our country club to swim for the day," she said. "Would you and your kids like to join us?"

Invitations like this didn't come very often. I drooled over the thought of sipping cold ice tea poolside and enjoying some meaningful adult conversation while my children splashed in a beautiful pool. But how would I ever get my house in shape?

On this particular day, I decided to go with the flow and take the kids swimming. I recognized that balancing people and tasks wasn't going to be an easy job, no matter how determined I was on a given day. But I also discovered there were ways to get things done ahead of time, leaving me a greater opportunity to develop rich relationships and do enjoyable activities along the way.

What Is Getting Organized and Simplifying Your Life?

Women know that "getting organized" is a great way to save time and avoid stress. But a desire to get there is often hindered by pressing duties and deadlines. Who really has time to get organized? After all, if we stopped everything we're doing to get organized, wouldn't that put us further behind? Not if you include simplifying your life as part of your plans.

Getting organized is like swatting mosquitoes on a summer day. You know the little creatures are bothering you, but their buzzing around never gets so bad that you have to stop what you are doing. When I hear someone say, "I've got to get organized," however, I know she is stressed and serious about changing. It's like a swarm of annoying mosquitoes has finally gotten to her, and she is ready to do something about it.

If too many bugs are buzzing around your ears, you can get organized in one of two ways:

- Organize and simplify "as you go" each day. For instance, straighten up the kitchen each night plus clean out one refrigerator shelf. In less than a week the whole refrigerator will be done.

- Set aside time to accomplish a bigger project. When something like reorganizing a closet means you have to pull things apart, schedule a half day to get the whole project done.

Simplifying your life is all about recognizing your problem areas and deciding which organizing system to use. Organizing is one of the things you do to simplify. Simplifying is the way to enjoy the manageable lifestyle you have organized at a reasonable pace. Do it as you go, or focus your efforts on one project at a time.

Where Do I Begin?

The basis of determining what to change is really quite simple: Keep what is working; change what is frustrating.

Let's begin by looking at the following vignettes that illustrate three powerfully important organizing principles. Let them stimulate your thinking of exactly how you want to make your life easier.

Organizing Principle #1: Make Your Organizing Memorable and Fun!

I had just finished speaking at a seminar in New York when a woman came running up to me.

"Do you remember me?" she uttered, a little out of breath. Before I could answer, she blurted out, "I'm Debbie, and I came to your seminar three months ago. Since then I have lost a hundred pounds!"

I didn't remember the woman, but I honestly could not imagine how this petite woman had lost so much weight.

"Wow!" I exclaimed. "That's amazing. Please tell me about it."

"After I came to your seminar three months ago, I cleaned out all my closets and my garage. I donated clothes, shoes, purses, and other unused items. Before I hauled it off to a charity, I bagged it all up and weighed everything—and it totaled one hundred pounds!"

Debbie and I shared a good laugh, and everyone around us congratulated her on her success. She had made her project fun by measuring her simplifying efforts in a tangible way. I am sure her energy and enthusiasm will carry over to her next household cleanup project, whether it's a pile of papers on her kitchen counter or a corner full of boxes stashed in the basement.

Success breeds success when it comes to good organization. And every victory counts toward the overall goal of simplifying your life.

Organizing Principle #2: Learn to Manage Your Current Situation with Ease

Adele was a competent attorney, having achieved her lifelong goal of working in a prestigious law firm. Her dreams began to vanish in a sleep-deprived fog, though, after she had her first baby. All her well-honed skills and strategies that kept her on top of the pack at work began to stall now that she was home.

"I don't know what's happened to me," she began. "I used to be organized, but it seems I've lost it all since I had my baby. The odd part is that even though I'm home all day, I can't seem to get anything done. I have only one month's leave from work left, but I wonder if I will ever get organized again. What's the matter with me?"

Inevitably, life changes for everyone with a new baby, an unforeseen job change, a new location, or an unexpected health issue. This can upset our rhythm until we regain our equilibrium and build a new lifestyle. Establishing a new purpose and a regular routine are the best solutions when life feels out of control.

In Adele's case, we began to rebuild her life one step at a time, recognizing that having a child and a career meant that life would not be the same as before. Knowing that she and the baby would take some time to adjust to each other, we started organizing the controllable—and familiar—part of her world, which was her work at the office.

We sorted piles of paper on her desk, credenza, and floor. She cleaned out her drawers and reorganized her files to accommodate her current work. I taught her to utilize a personal planner that included self-generated actions important to both her professional and personal life. She quickly learned that getting organized and staying organized was the key to maintaining the best of both worlds.

It takes courage and perseverance to restructure our time to handle the changes that come along in life. Adele could do that. As she adjusted to change, she gave herself permission not to take on anything new until she could manage her current situation with ease.

Organizing Principle #3: Use It or Lose It!

Lindsey came to my seminar, "Making a Clean Sweep in Your Home." Months later, she recognized me at a local grocery store.

"Marcia, I just have to tell you—your seminar saved my marriage."

"Really?" I asked in surprise. "I'm flattered you rate it so highly, but what do you mean exactly?"

"After you talked about getting rid of clutter and simplifying your life, I went home and got rid of all the 'stuff' that was sitting on my countertops, closets, floors . . . everywhere," she explained.

I smiled as I envisioned her progress from one countertop to the next and filling charity boxes with her overflowing items.

"We have three little girls under four years old," Lindsey continued. "My husband was always yelling at me about the mess in the house. Your seminar finally motivated me to get rid of everything we didn't use."

"Good for you, taking charge of your things!" I reaffirmed her.

Lindsey's eyes brightened. "After organizing for a couple weeks, my husband came home one day and said, 'I don't believe it. You really did it! This mess was driving me crazy, and I just couldn't keep living this way. It was about to destroy our marriage.'"

I gulped. "It's amazing how chaos can affect people."

"No kidding," Lindsey agreed. "I had no idea such a little thing could be such a big deal. Right then we sat down and talked—in the clean family room. After that I kept at it each day, and my husband even started to pitch in and help out. I'm not perfect, but now I feel so much better about my children, my marriage, and myself. Thank you!"

> **THREE ORGANIZING PRINCIPLES TO LIVE BY**
>
> 1. Make your organizing memorable and fun!
> 2. Learn to manage your current situation with ease.
> 3. Use it or lose it!

Lindsey's story is a dramatic example of how disorganization can hamper personal relationships and self-esteem. Instead of wallowing in self-pity over having three children under four years old, Lindsey got busy giving away extra toys, tossing piles of papers, and creating cleanup systems for the usual family "stuff" that litters a house every day. Getting rid of physical clutter always frees up time and space.

So remember this simple adage when you are looking at a pile of clutter: Use it or lose it. You don't have extra time or energy to waste on anything less important than the people you live with every day.

Life Worth More Than This

I don't promise that every organizing effort will yield a dramatic, life-changing result. But do you see my point? Your life is worth so much more than being tripped up by organizing issues. Organizing and simplifying your time, your home, and your work gives you more life to enjoy. Your life works for you when you have the right systems in place.

Three Key Questions before Making Any Change

Once you determine what it is that you want to change, it's easy to move that area into the limelight of your life and really begin to tackle it. To give you ideas, I'm showing you how three other women did it:

1. What is the desired outcome or goal?
   - Debbie: Organize and simplify her closets and garage.
   - Adele: Balance motherhood and work until they both worked.
   - Lindsey: Conquer the clutter and simplify her home.
   - You: _____

2. What are the next steps?
   - Debbie: Organize sections of her closet in the evenings and clean the garage on weekends.
   - Adele: Buy a planner and use it each day.
   - Lindsey: Simplify one room at a time and establish "pick-up" systems.
   - You: _____

3. What is your motivation to change?
   - Debbie: Driven by a personal desire to organize her "stuff."
   - Adele: Frustrated and anxious to balance work and motherhood.
   - Lindsey: Passionate to regain her self-esteem and control of her home.
   - You: _____

The Magic Key for Simplifying Your Life: The PuSH Sequence

Once you have answers to the above three questions, you're ready to simplify your life. After that, everything falls into a three-step sequence that I call "the PuSH Sequence." It is the key to getting organized and staying organized.

What Is the PuSH Sequence?

The PuSH Sequence is a three-step process to simplify any area of your life.

The first step: P=PROJECT—is a one-time planned organizing and simplifying event. A simplifying project can be cleaning out your closet, setting up a planner to manage your time, or drawing up a weekly chart to keep your home clean. A project is the foundation for building lasting change in one area. A project can take ten minutes

---

THE PuSH SEQUENCE FOR SIMPLIFYING YOUR LIFE

· ·

Step 1: P = PROJECT, a one-time focused investment to simplify an area of your life. The *u* in the PuSH Sequence is you and your style!

Step 2: S = SYSTEM, a dependable plan you set up to maintain the simplifying project you just completed.

Step 3: H = HABIT, a valuable personal routine you practice every day to stay organized.

---

or ten days to complete. The results repay you in time saved over and over after the initial investment.

The *u* in the PuSH Sequence is you!

All your simplifying and organizing systems need to reflect you, your personality, your role, and your sphere of influence. Every woman's life, family, work, and time are different. The more organized you get, the more your system should bring out the best of you.

For instance, if you work, your files and wardrobe should be professional and enjoyable. If you are a homemaker, then make your home a place of warmth and hospitality. If you want to excel at everything, then go ahead and work at it. If you tend to be lazy, then strategize your minimal work for dramatic results. If you are chronically ill, then focus on what you can do and not on what you can't do.

My motto is "Manage what you must, but organize what you care about . . . and what you're all about." You and your life are a treasure to polish and use to accomplish many wonderful things each day.

The second step: S = SYSTEM—is a simple plan to maintain the accomplished project every day. If it takes more than ten or fifteen minutes, it's too complicated and should be simplified.

For instance, keeping your closet organized should take no more than five minutes— time to hang up all your clothes and straighten the bedroom. Balancing your work and home should take no more than ten minutes to schedule tasks, meals, errands, and childcare for the next day. And cleaning up your home should take no more than fifteen minutes per area to put away each basket of laundry or toys in the family room once the initial organizing project is complete.

The third step: H=HABIT—is the key to staying organized because you're always doing things that work consistently well for you. These dependable, timesaving routines are the anchors that make life work no matter how busy you get. The chaos of life subsides when routine tasks move into dependable habits.

	P Project	u (You)	S System	H Habit
Debbie	• Clean out the closets after work and the garage on weekends.	• Take one day to go through your closet. • Ask a friend with good taste to come and help you make decisions.	• Organize clothes by category, color, and length, and create an attractive, functioning closet. • Put unused items in marked "giveaway" boxes.	• Put all clothes, shoes, and daily dressing items away each day. • Regularly recycle newspapers and giveaway items in the garage.
Adele	• Organize paperwork and time to balance the role of working mother.	• Find a personal planner or written system for a daily time schedule and task list.	• Use a personal planner with a daily and monthly calendar. • Complete projects in the time allotted.	• Plan tomorrow's activities before leaving work. • List tomorrow's errands and tasks before falling asleep.
Lindsey	• Learn how to keep a clutter-free home with three young children.	• Keep a smooth-running home by creating pick-up systems.	• Make beds each morning and put away laundry. • Give away extra items.	• Put away all toys before meals and clean up the kitchen right after meals. • Keep items that are useful to the family.

Will My Changes Make a Difference?

Whenever one person changes, other people around her should benefit. Some real-life client examples may help illustrate how your changes may make a difference:

- After being married for four years with clutter everywhere, Lisa decided to change. She wrote out a weekly chart just to get her laundry and cleaning done. When her cluttered house got cleaned up, her relatives began to praise her for the changes, and she began to enjoy her life at home for the first time.

- Dee Dee, a busy secretary in a large company, felt pulled in so many directions that she had chronic headaches. When she made one small change and consistently listed three priorities to accomplish at work each day, she started to get more things done. Her headaches subsided.

- When Chris, an experienced Bible study coordinator got a personal planner, she began to follow up on details and suggestions that came her way. In less than one year, the program doubled from 125 ladies to 250 because one person got a planner, started to plan ahead, and began to run her team like a leader.

Personal Reflection

Think back about our three ladies who made big changes. In Debbie's case, she lost 100 pounds by cleaning out the closets and garage. Adele organized her paperwork and purchased a personal planner to organize her limited time. Lindsey went through her house and conquered the daily clutter of three small children. All three women made progress by deciding what to do and taking action on their personal projects.

Now think about yourself. Take a few moments to reflect and answer the following questions.

1. What three areas do you most want to organize and simplify in your life? (Be as detailed as possible about what you want.)

_____

_____

_____

2. What steps could you take in that direction to give you dramatic and uplifting changes?

_____

_____

_____

3. What are all the good things that could possibly happen if you make that change?

_____

_____

_____

A Simple Prayer for Help

Dear God, I really would like to simplify my life, but I've tried before. This time help me actually do it, especially when I don't feel like it. Amen.

. . . .

Remember: Every day, some ordinary person does something extra-ordinary. Today, it's your turn.

—LOU HOLTZ, football coach

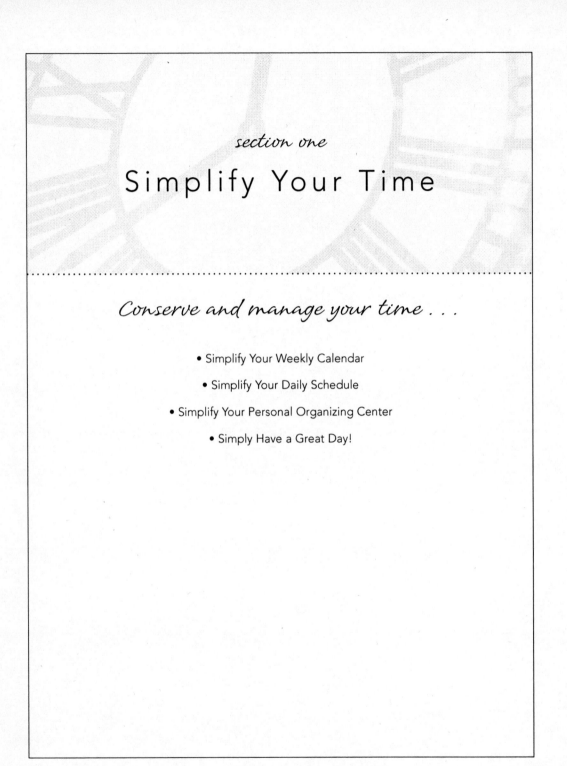

section one

Simplify Your Time

Conserve and manage your time . . .

- Simplify Your Weekly Calendar
- Simplify Your Daily Schedule
- Simplify Your Personal Organizing Center
- Simply Have a Great Day!

two

....

Simplify Your Weekly Calendar

The less clutter and commitments you have in your life, the less you'll feel pulled in so many different directions. When you simplify your life, you free up time.

—MICHELLE TULLIER, PH.D.
The Complete Idiot's Guide to Overcoming Procrastination

I love turning the page on a new calendar. Those white, pristine squares each month represent breathing room, margin in my life, and a relaxed pace. The reason I love them is simple—all that white space offers a chance to dream, an opportunity to change, and the potential to make those plans become a reality.

Can you change your life? Of course you can. And if you are to simplify your life, the best place to start is with your calendar, the place that creates the lifestyle you now live.

Time on your calendar reflects how you travel down the road of life, and there are two ways to view this passage of time. One way is to look at time *horizontally* from the beginning to the end of the week. We do this when we look at the Sunday-through-Saturday displays found on monthly calendars.

The other way is to look at time *vertically* for a single day from the beginning to the end. This is much like a long to-do list and set of appointments running from the top of the page to the bottom.

Whenever you feel the need to simplify your life, step back and view your calendar from both of these angles. Managing your time horizontally *and* vertically will help you beat the clock before time is up in a day.

Looking for Time?

When you manage time vertically, you race through the day like a 100-meter sprinter—either finishing winded and weary with leftover tasks, or winning the prize by finishing what you set out to do.

When you manage time horizontally, you rise above your schedule and set your sights on the week and month ahead. You understand the importance of conserving your energy for the long haul and pace yourself, much like a marathon runner.

The key to successful time management is evaluating your time from both angles. When you plan horizontally and vertically, you control your schedule, rather than allowing life's events to control you. Being proactive rather than reactive is a wonderful way to live.

↓ Organize Your Days Vertically

Managing time vertically means accomplishing the day's tasks in a time sequence from morning until night, the way they are written from top to bottom in the calendar square.

The Vertical Drop: Morning until Night

Martha, a working mother of two, was determined to catch up on life one Saturday morning. She began at 8 A.M. by reaching for a long to-do list taped to her refrigerator. By 10 A.M., she began to realize that her overly ambitious plans were nowhere near being completed.

"I had to do piles of laundry, clean the kitchen, get the mower fixed, and run four errands before I had to drive the kids to soccer practice and a birthday party," she lamented to me after that morning.

Martha began by glancing at her to-do list and surveying the housework awaiting her. *If my family would just help out, I wouldn't have to do all these things by myself,* she thought. She shook her head in frustration, retied her running shoes, and hit the errand trail.

Under pressure, we tend to fall into the same trap. Sometimes we even pull it off, but over time, we are doomed to frustration and feelings of perpetual catch-up if there is always too much to do in a day.

The solution I shared with Martha was not only to keep herself focused on the day's events vertically, but also to spread those tasks out horizontally over one week. Martha was a quick learner and rose to the challenge of recognizing how much she could realistically accomplish in a day. She got excited about checking things off during the week so her Saturdays could be more relaxed.

Viewing the Week and Month Ahead

A strategic way to pace yourself is to manage time from a horizontal perspective.

→ **Organize Your Days Horizontally**
Managing time horizontally means looking forward to the week and the month ahead to pace your schedule and energy accordingly.

Helen, a married physician with a large blended family and an active social life, learned horizontal management from trial and error. Now before she fills up an entire day and evening on her calendar, she looks over the week and month ahead to be sure that she has enough "breathing room" in her packed schedule.

It's not so much the number of commitments that can bog her down. Instead, it's the lack of "white space" on her calendar that can give her emotional breathing room to shift gears from one event to the next.

Helen has learned from her past mistakes that trying to handle her life and commitments in a perpetual hurry-up mode will leave her feeling frazzled. She now manages her time both horizontally and vertically and exudes a confidence and contentment that comes from feeling much more under control with her life's pace.

Managing time horizontally will improve your physical stamina and your emotional outlook for the long haul. This key to time management keeps your energy flowing smoothly, rather than taking a nosedive at the end of each day.

A Coming Crisis

I can tell when a crisis is coming just by looking at a woman's calendar. Scheduling wisely is the key to preventing chaos at home, burnout at work, and fatigue at the end of the day. The telltale clues in a woman's calendar predict whether she will thrive or just survive.

Brenda's Story

I remember meeting Brenda, a busy working woman, at one of my seminars. She asked for some advice. "I have a really busy schedule these days, but I promised to have my boss and his wife over soon. But I'm feeling stressed already."

"Do you have your monthly calendar with you?" I asked.

"Sure," she said. We happened to be in the first week of that month.

"Here's a good way to get started," I offered. "Let's look at the weekend nights first—Friday, Saturday, and Sunday—and see whether there is a problem there. Only two out of those three weekend evenings should be committed. It doesn't matter which night you take off, but you and your family need some down time, for at least one, if not two, of those evenings."

BRENDA'S CALENDAR

	SUNDAY	MONDAY	TUESDAY	WEDNESDAY	THURSDAY	FRIDAY	SATURDAY
WEEK 1			1 7–9 Class	2	3 4:30 Dentist	4	5 Groceries Wash 1 Football Game
WEEK 2	6 8:30 Worship	7 (Today!)	8 7–9 Class	9 5 Plumber	10 (Johnson's over?)	11 7:30 Banquet **1**	12 6 Dinner 8 Movie **2**
WEEK 3	13 8:30 Worship **(3)**	14 7 Committee **4**	15 7–9 Class **5**	16 7 School Open House **6**	17 6 Birthday Dinner **7**	18 —— Aunt Sally —— **8**	19 **9**
WEEK 4	20 8:30 Worship —— Aunt Sally —— **10**	21 (Crisis Day!)	22 7–9 Class	23	24 4:30 Haircut	25 Vacation Day!!!	26 8–4 CPR Training
WEEK 5	27 8:30 Worship 7 Musical	28	29 7–9 Class	30	31		

"Got it," said Brenda. "What about my weeknights?"

"From Monday through Thursday night, you should commit to having two of those four evenings free. Between weekends and weeknights, that means a maximum of four nights out per week."

When Brenda looked down at her calendar again, it was as if a light bulb went on. "One, two, three . . . oops," she said. "I'm planning to be out nine out of those ten nights!"

"Not a good idea," I said.

"But I already promised I'd have my boss and his wife over soon," Brenda pointed out. "What should I do?"

The Cost of a Busy Schedule

In Brenda's case, she really does have a time crisis brewing. If she follows through with her plans for the upcoming ten days, she will be heading toward a figurative crash landing. Like many women, she'll probably hold up well while going through it, but on the day after it's all over, watch out! That is when Brenda is likely to find herself irritable, discouraged, and emotionally burned out.

Calendar overload exacts a heavy price, which is why it's often not worth the "big push" to attend everything and please everyone. A calendar without breathing room wears any normal person out, so guard your calendar to reflect the pace of life that you can personally handle. Discouragement and fatigue may be a reflection of a time schedule out of balance.

When I pointed this out to Brenda, she immediately agreed that changes needed to be made. "Is there anything I can do about this pending time crunch?" she asked. "I can't let down my boss, Aunt Sally, or any of the committees I'm on. I'm just overbooked right now."

"We're just going to make some adjustments in that calendar of yours," I said. "If there's one good thing about a crisis, it's that it can help you see more clearly what the real priorities are."

Readjusting Your Calendar

The good news about Brenda's schedule is that adjustments could be made because everything was out in the future. We can learn some solutions from her busy calendar by noting the following ideas:

1. Ask your friends or boss if they could reschedule on a later date. Offer them two dates that would work better for both of you.
2. Schedule mutually enjoyable activities when out-of-town company arrives so you have something to look forward to as well.
3. Continue to participate in evening meetings, but let the chairman know ahead of time how long you plan to stay.
4. Reclaim one evening at home by covering your responsibilities in a one-on-one lunch meeting, by phone, or by e-mail with the leader.
5. Bottom line: Do yourself and others a favor by getting out of commitments when you're too busy to even be there.

Using a Calendar to Simplify Your Busy Life

Cherish your time by treating your personal calendar as a prized possession. Keep your calendar with you at all times, if possible. Having your appointments, meeting plans, and phone numbers close by will help you successfully manage any changes that come up.

The way you schedule events can simplify or complicate your life, so remember these tips:

1. Keep one monthly calendar.
2. Write down all your appointments in one or two words.
3. Diagonally mark off passed date boxes while reflecting if it was time well spent.
4. Pencil in all appointments and potential events coming up.
5. Promptly say no to invitations and meetings that you cannot or do not wish to attend.
6 Always respond to everyone who contacts you, if possible.
7. Offer two alternative options when rescheduling an event.
8. Leave a large portion of your Sunday open for worship and restful activities.

One Life, One Calendar

Most women have many parts to their lives and more than one calendar to manage them. This can be a problem. If you have a calendar on the refrigerator, one in your purse, and one at work, you're going to be one overscheduled woman. The worst part is that you'll be leaving out the most important commodity to make it all work—you.

There are only twenty-four hours in anyone's day, and you don't need to add to your stress by feeling fragmented and having things fall through the cracks. Your calendar—a single calendar—should reflect a balanced and satisfying life for you. You can start that journey by consolidating your activities through living one life on one calendar.

Detecting a Pattern

Your calendar contains many clues. If the early part of your week goes well but you are frustrated by the end of the week, look at your schedule from prior weeks and determine if you can detect a pattern. Seeing what a "good day" looks like on that day of the week will help you choose the way you schedule things.

Skimming, a Red Flag

When hectic days come, a woman finds herself skimming to just hit the priorities. Skimming at work means a never-ending in-box and unreturned messages, while at home, mail, laundry, and dishes pile up. Before she knows it, she is overstressing herself and resenting the life she once enjoyed.

If this is your situation, stop the chaos and deal with the annoying details by canceling something in your schedule. Having the courage to say "no" to too much activity keeps your life from spiraling out of control.

Building Flexibility into Planning

The woman who needs to be out evenings can lower her stress by pacing herself through the three parts of every day—morning, afternoon, and evening. A good rule of thumb is to make one part of the day a time to regroup and have some personal down time.

See these other examples of flexible planning:

- A working woman finds she is tired and fatigued every Monday morning because her weekend was too busy. She needs to rearrange her weekends so that she can enter the workweek refreshed.

- A mother, noticing that her preschoolers balk at going to preschool activities every day from Monday through Friday, may decide to cut back to only three preschool days per week.

• A teenager is fatigued from beginning his high-school classes at 7:10 A.M. A look at his weekly calendar may reveal the need to reduce the number of extracurricular activities that force him to stay up late at night.

Husband's Patterns

As I observed patterns in my family, I noticed a glaring one in my husband's schedule.

"David, what happens on Thursdays at work? They seem to be more stressful for you," I inquired one evening.

My husband paused defensively, looked at me, and said, "Thursdays are just like any other day. What makes you say that?"

"Well, honey, every weeknight you come home at about the same time, but on Thursdays you come home late and stressed. What happens on Thursdays?" I asked again.

After giving the question some thought and checking his calendar, he said, "I have regular weekly meetings scheduled every hour, all day long on Thursdays. So I have to stay late to get some of my own work done. Hmm. Maybe I should shift some of the meetings to another day."

"Maybe you should do that," I said evenly.

"I think I will!"

Planning horizontally has many benefits. You can even find time for yourself by scheduling an appointment named "My Time" or "Family Time" and writing it in like any other appointment.

Time is not flexible, but your schedule is. Figure out what works for you and the people in your life. Then guard these priorities carefully on your monthly calendar.

Teach Your Family to Plan Ahead

You can teach your family to plan time together by gathering over Saturday brunch or a "pizza calendar party" every Sunday night. This built-in family time allows you to discuss what's ahead and create ways to spend time together in the coming week.

Ask about their work and sports schedules as well as their ideas for dinners. Talk through each day of the week until you get to the next weekend. This way you can calendar the family events, even if you are the only one to show up with a pen in hand.

Help your family count the nights out per week to avoid overextending themselves.

An overcommitted calendar is the quickest way to drain all the enthusiasm and momentum from your life, as well as the lives of your spouse and children. Organize and revitalize your family with a good plan for the week ahead.

TIME TIPS FOR FAMILY LIVING

Try these time tips for less stressful family living:

Toddlers: Be five minutes ahead of them. Otherwise your day will begin with a downward spiral as you sleepily eye the messy kitchen and hear your little ones proudly announce, "Mommy, we made breakfast!"

School-aged children: Be one hour ahead of them. Remind them of what is next—whether school, music, or sports—so they can mentally start to transition and collect what is needed.

Teenagers: Be one day ahead of them. If your teenager wants the car on the weekend, leverage his motivation by requiring that he clean his room and do chores beforehand.

Husband: Be three months ahead of him. If you want to get the house painted in the summer, start selecting colors in the spring. Discuss what you want to accomplish and when you can best do it. The same goes for a summer vacation, because a one- or two-week trip takes a lot of advanced planning.

Retiring Spouse: Be one year ahead of him. Months ahead of retirement, initiate discussions about projects you want to tackle together, or exciting trips you hope to take during your "golden years." This is the time to work together as a team for mutual enjoyment.

Plan Tomorrow the Night Before

Planning tomorrow the night before means confirming tomorrow's time schedule. This may mean that you need to confirm appointments and carpools, get directions, and write out your to-do list the night before. You will likely find that people are prepared for appointments and more enthusiastic about get-togethers if you take a few minutes to confirm things the day before.

Each evening, take the time to gather your purse and things you need for the next day—packages to be mailed, new purchases to be returned, and dry cleaning to be dropped off—in one launching spot. This will help you avoid the last-minute stress of collecting things.

You can also simplify life by tacking on one errand at the end of a workday or an appointment to free up your weekends for more enjoyable events. You will be more productive and happy if you create larger blocks of time to spend on things you enjoy.

The PuSH Sequence for Getting Your Calendar Together

1. What's the problem?
   - Martha: Too many things to do on Saturday.
   - Brenda: Stressed about the upcoming ten days.
   - You: _____

2. What's the goal?
   - Martha: Get more things done with limited time.
   - Brenda: Have the boss and his wife over and not be stressed.
   - You: _____

3. What are the next action steps?
   - Martha: Spread tasks over a week and be realistic about Saturday.
   - Brenda: Count nights and cut back on the busiest weeks of activities and appointments.
   - You: _____

Put *u* in the PuSH System for simplified living by choosing a personal planner that you like to look at and writing down everything that's in your schedule. Let it reflect all the people and things you value.

··

Remember: Plan tomorrow the night before.
And use the weekend to plan the next two weeks ahead.

··

	P ──────▶ Project	u ──────▶ (You)	S ──────▶ System	H Habit
Martha	• Manage time vertically by thinking through how to get all tasks done in a day.	• Put everything on the calendar and keep it in the same spot every day.	• Plan tomorrow the night before by calling ahead, gathering items, and cleaning up papers and clutter.	• Every night write out the plans for the following day. • Keep priorities based on their results.
Brenda	• Manage time horizontally for the week ahead for balance.	• Find a personal planner or written system for a daily time schedule and task list.	• Look for patterns of good days and weeks. Repeat them. • Cut out activities until balance can be achieved.	• On the weekend, evaluate the two weeks ahead. • Make commitments based on horizontal planning, not just available white space.

Personal Reflection

Look ahead as you scrutinize your calendar vertically for overcommitted days and horizontally for imbalanced weeks.

To make sure you don't run out of energy before your day is over, look at your monthly calendar right now and take the following steps:

- Mark off the days that have passed this month with a diagonal slash.
- Add all the events you know are coming up.
- Put a check mark after the week where four nights are already committed.
- Add or delete any events to reflect a lifestyle you thrive in for the next two months.
- Repeat events if you like them.

For best results, only plan up to 70 percent of your time with a 30 percent time cushion for the unexpected. Be aware that planning too little activity can result in boredom, so don't go overboard and cut out too much.

A Simple Prayer for Strength

Dear God, You know my life, and You know how much I can handle in a day. Please help me to organize my time so I can accomplish all that is in front of me. Gently remind me in stressful times to quiet my heart with a quick prayer so I can draw upon Your great strength to help me. Amen.

. . . .

The people who are most successful in managing their time make appointments with themselves to complete tasks.

—BARBARA HEMPHILL, *Taming the Paper Tiger*

three

....

Simplify Your Daily Schedule

Just as you can fit only so much into a closet or drawer, you can fit only so much into your waking hours.

—JULIE MORGENSTERN
Time Management from the Inside Out

Since managing time is the key to managing your life, it's important to get the most out of each day. Each sunrise offers a new opportunity to rearrange your time, meet with interesting people, and schedule purposeful activities. But there is only so much you can fit into any one twenty-four-hour period, no matter what your aspirations are.

The goal to simplifying life includes finding better ways to choose what you want to do, looking for opportunities to reduce your stress, and ending the day with more things done than undone. As one of my favorite quotes says, "It is not the things we do that make us tired; it is the things left undone that wear us out."

Putting together all the tasks in a woman's day is like putting together a puzzle. When the goal is to get things done and still enjoy the day, we need to put our best foot forward. Even with all our multitasking talents as women, we know that life can get complicated and crazy. Is there an easier way to do it? I believe there is, especially if you can acquire a new perspective to deal with each day.

After talking about managing our week horizontally in the last chapter, it's time to look at managing each day vertically, from morning until night.

Sue's Dilemma

I met Sue when I went to organize her office. Instead of starting on her paper piles, she poured out her most recent frustration—starting at home.

I'm not a morning person. Actually I dread mornings. That is when the chaos of my day begins.

Yesterday was especially bad when my daughter, Alyssa, asked me at breakfast where the three dozen cookies were that she was taking in for her teacher's going-away party. I had totally forgotten to bake them, and I had a meeting with my boss at 8 A.M. I was twenty minutes late.

Besides disappointing my daughter and my boss, my best friend's birthday crept up on me. I even bought her card and present early, but I couldn't find either of them. I felt as though I had failed again.

My son, Jimmy, needed his white shirt ironed for his first band concert. I couldn't find time to iron it. On top of that, the house was a mess, and it frustrated me that I had to squeak out the last bit of toothpaste before bed the night before. I haven't had time to get to the store.

I wanted to sit down and cry, but I didn't even have time for that. So I grabbed the back of an envelope and scribbled out all the things I needed to remember. And I vowed that I would make some serious changes.

So here I am. What should I do?

Climbing Out of Chaos

Sue was in a definite time crunch, and by 7 A.M., her stress level had zoomed into high gear. Life had piled up around her. And she finally recognized it that morning. It was time for a change.

All her good intentions of being a good mom, a loyal friend, and a good employee were falling apart—over what? Over unbaked cookies, a misplaced birthday present, a late arrival at work, no toothpaste, and a shirt to iron!

Sue has organizational issues to conquer, not character flaws to sabotage her sense of well-being. To simplify her disorganized day, we started by restructuring her mornings.

Four Time-Management Lifestyles

Without realizing it, most women operate under one of four time-management methods. It is important that you understand which system you use most and be able to bring others into the mix when you need to ease your time stressors.

The four styles, described below, progress from simple to detail oriented. They work well for a variety of situations but fail us at others. Perhaps you will recognize where you are now and how you can move forward to more peace and order.

You don't want your life to fall apart just because you forgot to buy toothpaste, just as you don't want such a simple task to become the priority of your day. If enough loose ends are not handled at the right time, a minor "one more thing" could be your undoing. A crisis is a signal to slow down and consciously choose a better system.

At any rate, let's take a closer look at the four time-management styles:

1. *The crisis and memory method*: The crisis and memory method reacts to urgent items and relies on memory, two things that usually don't work well together. The crisis and memory method is reactive, not proactive. It can work well if you have a great memory and can do immediately whatever crosses your mind. Many women, however, find this impulsive style frustrating because they change directions way too often since they haven't planned ahead. This frustrates other family members as well.

That's how Sue reacted when so many things came at her all at once. She ran into trouble when her memory failed under the stress of everything happening at once. Her life became a traffic jam of deadlines before she even left the house. Not a good situation.

2. *The list and pile method*: The list and pile system shows more preparation, but it depends on visual reminders such as items laid out on counters—plus lists, schedules, and appointment cards plastered to the refrigerator.

Sue could actually have benefited from this method by having a "launching spot" each night where she and the family lined up fresh-baked cookies, backpacks filled with homework and schoolbooks, and an ironed band outfit from left to right in order of the next day's events.

The list and pile method works if there are only one to three items lined up in order of the day's events, but it fails when the items sit there for more than a day.

A Word about Lists

I asked Sue to write out a to-do list for that morning. While making a list is a step in the right direction, it only gets you halfway there. So let's examine Sue's list and see if she could have done better:

- First, write out a list (this would be a 50 percent improvement).
  Bake three dozen cookies for Alyssa's teacher
  Drop off Diane's birthday present
  Wash and iron Jimmy's band shirt
  Buy toothpaste
  Jimmy's first band concert
  Clean the family room and kitchen

- Next, insert times and rearrange the list in time sequence (this would be an 80 percent improvement).

  Sue would be better off adding times to her to-do list, stating her action steps in a few words, and beginning each action step with an action verb. Under normal circumstances, she could have a Plan A list, but in times of crisis, she'd need to create a Plan B as illustrated below.

Plan A: Reasonable Plan

Evening before: bake or buy cookies
Evening before: wash Jimmy's band shirt
7:25 A.M.: drop kids and cookies at school
Noon: take Diane's birthday present
4:30 P.M.: buy toothpaste
6:45 P.M.: attend Jimmy's concert
Saturday: clean the family room and kitchen

Plan B: Crisis Mode Plan

7:00 A.M.: buy at grocery store:

1. cookies

2. toothpaste

3. birthday card for Diane

4. Starbucks gift card for Diane

7:20 A.M.: drive kids and cookies to school

7:25 A.M.: take Jimmy's shirt to dry cleaners

7:50 A.M.: arrive at work for meeting

11:45 A.M.: Diane's lunch at Olive Garden

5:40 P.M.: pick up shirt at dry cleaners

6:00 P.M.: dinner of leftovers

6:45 P.M.: Jimmy's first band concert

Saturday: clean the family room and kitchen

- Now live it (resulting in 100 percent success)!

With practice, this system will become second nature as Sue writes tasks down in a logical time sequence. She won't have to recopy anything. And she will learn what activities work best at certain times of the day. A good time manager learns and guards these time slots.

3. *The calendar method:* Difficulties arise when the only organization system used is a family wall calendar, a small one in a purse, or a desk blotter with telephone numbers and notes scribbled in the margins.

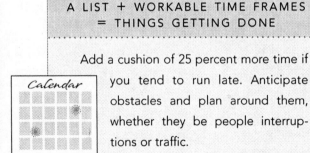

A LIST + WORKABLE TIME FRAMES = THINGS GETTING DONE

Calendar

Add a cushion of 25 percent more time if you tend to run late. Anticipate obstacles and plan around them, whether they be people interruptions or traffic.

With the calendar method, you may be able to write down all your appointments, but you will miss errands, self-initiated tasks, and phone calls because they're scribbled on the margin of the calendar or on the refrigerator that you can't take with you.

That's why women should consider using the next method.

4. *The planner method:* A planner is a book with sections to organize your activities and

lists. It is basically everything you need to stay organized all in one place. It is a system for people who have numerous details to attend to or who never have the same day twice.

Whether it is a program on your computer, an electronic PDA (Personal Digital Assistant), or a calendar-type book you take with you, a personal planner has significantly improved the lives of many busy women.

SUE'S DAY IN A PLANNER

	TIME EVENTS	TO DO
7:00	❑ Wash whites	3 PRIORITY PROJECTS
	❑ Find birthday card	A1 ❑ Diane's birthday today!
8:00	❑ Deliver cookies	
		A2 ❑ Wash whites!!!
9:00		
	8–3	A3 ❑ Phone calls
10:00	**Work**	
11:00		
noon	Birthday lunch ❑ Make calls	
1:00		CALLS:
		❑ Reschedule meeting
2:00		❑ RSVP Sat. dinner
3:00	❑ Pick up dry cleaning ❑ Put away laundry	
4:00	4–5 Soccer ❑ Toothpaste	
5:00		AT HOME TO DO:
	5:30 Dinner	❑ Wash whites!!!
6:00		
7:00	**7:00 Jimmy's band concert**	
		DISCUSS WITH SPOUSE:
8:00		❑ RSVP Sat. dinner
	❑ Down time to relax	
9:00	❑ Plan tomorrow on paper	

Fill in the Night Before:
1 ✓ TIME EVENTS
2 ✓ CALLS
3 ✓ ERRANDS
4 ✓ PRIORITY PROJECTS

TO-DO LIST (10 items):
✓ Take 3 doz. cookies
   (school)
✓ Diane's birthday today!
✓ Work/Activities 8–3
✓ Drive to soccer (4–5)
✓ Dinner (5:30)
✓ Sale: Toothpaste/Scope
✓ Reschedule meeting
   (6 people)
✓ Wash whites!!!
✓ Jimmy's 1st band concert
✓ RSVP Sat. dinner

A planner is like having a personal assistant always with you. Nothing is missed because everything is in one spot. Priorities are written down in the right place, and life's details are simplified.

My rule of thumb is that if everything won't fit on one page in your planner, then you can't live it all out in one day.

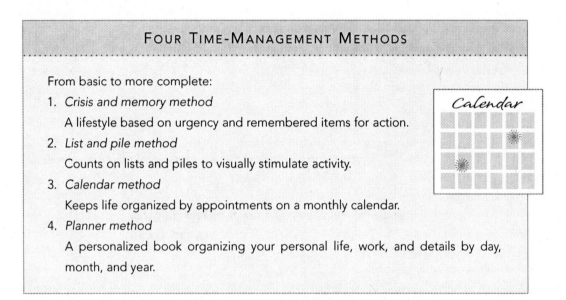

FOUR TIME-MANAGEMENT METHODS

From basic to more complete:

1. *Crisis and memory method*
   A lifestyle based on urgency and remembered items for action.
2. *List and pile method*
   Counts on lists and piles to visually stimulate activity.
3. *Calendar method*
   Keeps life organized by appointments on a monthly calendar.
4. *Planner method*
   A personalized book organizing your personal life, work, and details by day, month, and year.

Choices Even in Chaos

For Sue, simplifying her days comes down to adjusting her systems. I showed her that she could do better than running her life from the back of an envelope. She agreed to get a planner and place a pad of paper by each telephone at home so she could at least organize her thoughts on something better than the back of an envelope.

That night she was on her way to a smoother morning the next day when

- the whole family relaxed and celebrated Jimmy's first concert with ice cream afterward;
- together they laid out items for the next day;
- Sue took the time to itemize tomorrow's to-dos, phone calls, and errands;
- Sue rearranged the next day in time order on paper before falling asleep.

Sue's list is like any woman's list these days. We all have similar things that need to get done: urgent, necessary, and postponable. Deciding what must get done and strategically doing it at the best time keeps us moving forward in life. Personal organization comes down to deciding which method to use to make all the strategic details of life happen.

Personal Evaluation

1. Right now I use the following methods (check):
   ❏ Crisis and memory method
   ❏ List and pile method
   ❏ Calendar method
   ❏ Planner method

2. I could really improve if _____

....

The palest ink is better than the best memory.
—CHINESE PROVERB

....

CHOOSING A PLANNER

You can keep your monthly calendar and daily to-do lists in a planner or electronic organizer. Choose it as carefully as you would an important everyday accessory, like a watch or purse. Remember these tips:

1. Choose a planner that is right for you. The three basic sizes include

   • Portable size (3 x 6 inches)
   • Half-sheet size (5 x 8 inches)
   • Large folio (8 x 11 inches)

Choose a style and color that best suits your personality. Keep in mind that a leather cover looks professional, and a canvas cover is casual. Buy the one you can picture yourself using every day.

If you decide to use an electronic version of a planner—the handheld PDA—get one that you've previewed and that suits your needs.

2. Include these items to simplify your time and life.
   - Monthly calendar. Separated by tabs, each month should lie across one or two pages. These monthly calendars provide the big picture of your life for the whole year.
   - Daily pages. The daily page gives you the space to list appointments chronologically, record tasks, and make notes to capture all your plans for the day in an orderly fashion.
   - Address and phone section. This is a key for saving enormous amounts of time because all your addresses, home phone numbers, cell phone numbers, and even store hours and directions are in one place.
   - Attach a pen and pencil. Use a pencil to write down appointments and meetings on your monthly calendar and a pen to write everything else.

Keep your personal planner propped open on your counter at home or on your desk at work, and list all the action items mulling around in your mind. Read it often. Check off completed items, and feel free to rearrange your time on paper to get the most out of your day.

If you want to know what day it is, any calendar will do. But if you want to gain control of your time, schedule priority tasks, and gain a reputation for getting things done, use a planner!

—HAROLD TAYLOR, *Making Time Work for You*

Test Your Organizational Skills

Sometimes taking an honest look at our activities and lifestyle gives us clues for saving time and reducing stress. In this exercise, write "yes" or "no" next to each question to pinpoint certain stressful areas:

_____ 1. Do you know how long it takes you and your family to get up and out the door each morning?

_____ 2. Do you lower your stress by arriving on time or early for your appointments?

_____ 3. Do you stay current by returning calls and e-mails the same day?

_____ 4. Have your bills and credit cards been paid on time for the past six months?

_____ 5. Do you know how much money you have in your purse and bank accounts?

_____ 6. Do you know how much gas you have in the tank? Is your car clutter free?

_____ 7. Are all clean clothes put away and all the dirty clothes in the hamper?

_____ 8. Do you know what's for dinner and how long it will take to make it?

_____ 9. Would people say you are organized?

_____10. Do you *feel* organized?

Bonus question:

_____ Did you organize and simplify something in your life in the last three weeks?

Score: 10 points for each "yes" response, plus five points for the bonus question.

Results:

- 90 points or higher. Congratulations! You have excellent organization skills, and you could be giving seminars on this topic.

- 70–80 points. You're a generally well-organized person who has things together.

- 50–60 points. You're a little organized, and that's what I'm afraid of—you're just a little organized.

- 10–40 points. Uh-oh. Life's getting the best of you. You are going to be a big hit with your improvements.

Twenty-One Times to a New Lifestyle

We must continue to refine our systems so everything works for us and not against us each day. New habits need to be done at least twenty-one times the new way before they become a habit. It may take you longer than twenty-one days to make a new habit, but it's worth the effort. If you are committed to simplifying your life, polish your good habits and overcome your lazy ones.

Ten Timesaving Habits to Simplify Your Day

The faster the pace of your life, the more organized you need to be. Simplify your life by mastering these ten timesaving habits.

1. Make your bed and make your day. It takes only two minutes to give you sixteen hours of order. Besides, a room is 50–70 percent clean when the bed is made.

2. Practice the "two-minute pick-up" every time you leave a room or your desk. Before you leave a room, turn around and quickly put away everything for two minutes. The more you put away before you leave, the smoother your transition when you return.

3. Learn to love clean counters. Cluttered counters represent undone actions. Significant amounts of time and energy are lost if dishes, mail, children's papers, and clutter are not dealt with or neatly put away.

4. Cut your work in half by putting things away now. One of the biggest time wasters is saying, "I'll deal with that later." Put everything away now.

5. Set the pace for your day by arriving early, or at least on time, at your first event. Your arrival time at the first event often sets the pace for the rest of your day. Stress less by arriving on time.

6. Be sure dinner is on time and regular. Late dinners throw everyone out of whack— late baths, late homework, and late chores. Have dinner at a time that still gives you plenty of day left to get things done and plan for tomorrow.

7. Solve the problem of "I forgot . . ." Don't clutter your mind with things to remember. Write them down in your planner and review it frequently.

8. Assign to-do items to the three days you have most control over: today, tomorrow, and the next day. Life has a way of filling up quickly, so try to do each item promptly. Also, limit your lists to ten items so that you don't get overwhelmed.

9. Strive to focus your day's events on things you enjoy. You will enjoy the things you like to do a lot more if you get other things done in a timely and orderly fashion.

10. Congratulate yourself daily for your accomplishments. Use positive self-talk during the day. And if you go through your day with a smile and a good attitude, you get bonus points for brightening up the world.

	P Project	u (You)	S System	H Habit
Sue	• Conquer the morning routine.	• Get a planner and get ahead each night.	• List to-dos in a time sequence. • Combine down time and family time each evening.	• End each day planning the next day. • Lay out items the night before.
You	• Decide what time habits are hindering you regularly.	• Change the most frustrating times in your day.	• Set out to improve one habit for one entire month.	• Get better each day at accomplishing what you intend to do.

Personal Reflection

If you are happy and productive, that is good. But if your days leave you flat and frustrated, then you need a new approach. Why is that? You've fallen into routine patterns, and you're running through your daily maze the same old way.

But there is hope. If you are always late, rushed, or behind on things, there are ways to get organized, become productive, and feel peaceful about your day. There is an art to getting things done and still enjoying what you want to.

Answer "yes" or "no" to the following questions as you think about your own life.

_____ 1. Do you run out of time before your day is over?
_____ 2. Were any of your stresses in recent days caused by transition time from one event to another?
_____ 3. Are you living your days predominantly vertically or horizontally?
_____ 4. Can you think of any way to adjust your schedule to make life easier?

Well-Managed Days

Since time is not flexible, the first step in creating smoother days is to control your calendar in a more purposeful manner. Plan ahead from morning until night (vertically) for each day and pace yourself for the week and month ahead (horizontally). Conquer your problem areas and celebrate your improvements.

A Simple Prayer for Wisdom

Dear God, sometimes my life is so fast paced that I can't get off the treadmill of busyness. Other times life is slow and I feel bored and lonely. Help me to be wise and balance each day better than the day before. And thank You that I do have more choices than I think I do. Amen.

. . . .

We must always uncover the "time bandits" and the "time robbers" that we are allowing to cheat us out of our valuable minutes. Then, once they are identified, we must guard against them because they can so easily seize our minutes and sap us of our precious life!

—Elizabeth George, *Life Management for Busy Women*

four

Simplify Your Personal Organizing Center

*Clutter is postponed decisions.® Ask yourself, "What is the next action
I need to take on this piece of paper?"*

—BARBARA HEMPHILL
Taming the Paper Tiger

I remember when Jamie made her distress call to me. "I can't seem to keep up with all the paper in my life," she lamented. "The piles just keep growing. I've got a stack of mail that never seems to go away, receipts to file, good articles to read, and important notes scribbled to myself on pieces of scratch paper. Then there's the kids' papers, my husband's stuff, and who knows what else. The only good thing is that I manage to keep my bills in one spot," said Jamie.

"So far, how have you been trying to handle your paperwork?" I queried.

"I guess I'm the typical 'paper piler.' When a pile of mail gets too big, I hide it out of sight just in case I might need something. I must have five grocery bags of paperwork stuffed in my pantry. I don't have time to go through it all, but I always worry that something important is in there."

"Well," I said, "the good news about those papers is that most of them are probably expired, so they're going to be easy to toss. But what you really need is a system to keep you from falling back into the old out-of-sight routine."

"I do need help," Jamie agreed. "So how do I get it under control? This is my biggest problem, and I am always stressed out about it."

A Personal Organizing Center

For Jamie and most women like her, there is nothing more distressing than facing a mail pile on the kitchen counter. Getting the growing pile of papers under control is always difficult, but once it's done, you can breathe a huge sigh of relief and know you've taken a positive step to simplify life.

Managing time is hard enough, but when you add a mound of paperwork to the mix, it can become overwhelming. One way to push through those paper piles and time-related tasks is to set up a personal organizing center—a "command central" to organize yourself and your life.

Now I know what you are thinking: What in the world is a personal organizing center, and how will I ever fit one into my home? Let me reassure you that you already have a semblance of a personal organizing center, or POC, in your home at your kitchen counter by your phone. It's time to fine-tune this location so you can orchestrate your calendar, the mail, events, and projects that come your way. If you handle the POC well, you are well on your way to simplifying your life.

It is there that the newly organized woman with her planner handles all the incoming mail with easy access to a calendar, telephone, and supply drawer. It is there that every piece of paper for the day flows through and decisions are made.

Location, Location, Location

Your personal organizing center is generally a two-foot-square space on the kitchen counter and near a telephone. This is the place where, when you walk in the door, you drop your purse, dump the mail, store the day's papers, and generally "work" your home. It's here that you look at your calendar during the day, check the telephone for voice messages, find out where the kids need to be next, return phone calls, prepare a grocery list, decide what to cook for dinner, and update your husband about what's happening.

Why the kitchen? The kitchen is the room from which your life flows. The kitchen is more than a place where you cook meals and do dishes; it's a place where you keep your life organized. The kitchen truly is the heart of the home. It should be the cleanest and most clutter-free room in your house.

Set It Up Right

1. *Location:* A woman's personal organization center is where she opens the daily mail. It could be a kitchen counter with a single drawer containing neatly organized desk supplies and a kitchen cabinet shelf above it. It should include the following elements:

   - Telephone
   - Desk supplies
   - A calendar

2. *Activities:* Without realizing it, you can handle seven different time and paper activities in your kitchen. How many of these tasks are part of your kitchen right now?

   - Handling today's mail
   - Centralizing all calendar events
   - Answering the phone
   - Returning voice messages
   - Calling friends
   - Making appointments
   - Arranging carpools and schedules

3. *Time:* When is the best time to work at your personal organizing center? Four times during the day are equally effective:

   - At the beginning of the day
   - When the mail comes in
   - Before or after meals
   - At the end of the day

Fifteen Pieces of Mail a Day

Did you know that each day an average of fifteen pieces of mail arrive in your mailbox? If you flip through and deal with only ten of the fifteen pieces, you are left with five dangling pieces a day to be dealt with later. That's why stacks of mail can appear from out of nowhere. At the rate of five pieces of mail per day, that means 130 pieces a month or 1,565 pieces a year—sixteen inches of guilt piled on your desk or countertops. Help!

Two Paperwork Goals

As you process your time and paper activities, remember the following goals:

Goal 1: Take action on the papers that you need or want. Toss the rest!

Goal 2: Work until the counter is clear. Keep working the papers until they're done, filed, or tossed.

Remember, loose papers represent undone actions. They drain emotional energy and take away your peace of mind.

Where to Begin

Walk into your kitchen right now and survey the counters for stray papers. Then investigate the refrigerator door, the eating area, and any other catchalls around the house for stray papers. Has your paper trail started to overtake your household without your even realizing it? If so, you can start doing something about it right now.

Determine to open the mail in one spot in your home. I highly recommend that you make that place your new kitchen personal organizing center. Don't even think about carrying your mail to the family room, living room, bedroom, bathroom, or car.

Keep your planner open in front of you as you open the mail. This enables you to quickly jot down calendar events, action steps, and addresses.

Keep your desk supplies in a drawer or decorative box nearby when you open your mail. This includes a divided tray with your letter opener, paper clips, scissors, and Scotch tape. Keep some manila or colored file folders nearby that you can file necessary paperwork in. Then file everything in a file cabinet or portable file box (preferably out of sight).

Speed up the mail process by standing at the counter. If you plop yourself in a comfortable chair or couch in the living room, you'll be comfortable all right, but less productive than if you handle all the paper standing up.

Picture This

The mail has been delivered. So what are you going to do once you've carried that mail from the mailbox to the personal organizing center?

First, turn over the pile of mail and slit it open with a letter opener (unless it's some junk mail, like another credit card come-on, that you can confidently toss right into the recycle bin or shredder). Using a letter opener is more efficient and eliminates the jagged edges left behind when you use your finger to open the envelopes.

Now that your mail is opened upside down, pick up the first piece. Because you are probably looking at a blank side of paper, you are increasing the curiosity factor to see what's inside—like an unopened present. Turn it over and toss the envelope into the garbage. Now anticipate how you will deal with the contents by keeping the following four rules in mind.

The Four Rules of Handling Paper

Rule 1: Immediately list, file, or toss every paper you don't need on your counter (such as calendar events, advertisements, or flyers).

Rule 2: Do paper-generating tasks immediately if it takes five minutes or less (to call, to order, to read).

Rule 3: List action steps for important papers in your planner or on a master list before placing them in your to-do file.

Rule 4: Simplify your life and do some of those important actions on your desk list today.

If you do this each day, it should take only ten to twenty minutes to reclaim your clean counter from paper piles.

Be Decisive about Paper

If you get stuck not knowing what to do with a piece of paper, or if you are tempted to put it down in a pile, stop. Hold the paper and answer these questions until you take action:

1. Am I willing to give up time and space to follow through on this piece of paper?
2. What action does this piece of paper require, and when will I do it?
3. Do I really want or need this piece of paper?

The key to simplifying paper is to be decisive when you first look at a paper. If you act decisively, you should easily be able to toss 70 percent of the paper coming into your home on the same day.

What to Do with the Extra Papers

If the mail coming your way is in one of the following categories, handle it as suggested below, but deal with it until it is all put away. Assume there is a way to file it instead of piling it, and keep working until you find a system that works for you and looks nice.

Small Drawer in Counter or Desk

File by size: Place small papers vertically in a drawer and $8\frac{1}{2}$-by-11-inch papers unfolded in a file folder.

- *Bills.* Toss the advertising inserts, review the bill, place it under the flap of the return envelope, and set it in your bill container (or drawer) that's within reach.

- *Coupons.* Selectively cut coupons and file them away in an attractive and easy-to-use coupon holder, which should be kept in a drawer until going to the supermarket.

The PuSH Sequence for Getting It Together

	P Project	u (You)	S System	H Habit
Bills	• Toss envelopes and fliers. • Check for accuracy. • Write the due date where the stamp goes.	• Find a regular time each week to deal with financial matters.	• Place a bill in a drawer or holder. • Keep stamps and checkbook nearby. • Set up automatic payments or pay online.	• Pay bills one day each week, or on the 1st and 20th of the month. • Review all income and expenses. • Transfer funds for higher interest.
Coupons	• Clip coupons at the same time and place. • Time how long coupon clipping takes and compare it to the financial gain.	• Decide the best way for you to get more for your time and money on groceries.	• File coupons in labeled sections of a coupon holder. • Keep coupons in a drawer, not clipped on the fridge—messy!	• Take coupons to the store. • Toss less desirable and expired coupons each time you file.

File Folder 1: CALENDAR

Important: Do not put an item in the CALENDAR file until you pencil it in on your monthly calendar in your planner. This folder is invaluable to clean up paper piles by holding related papers until the date comes and you need it.

- *Invitations.* Check your calendar. If it is an event you want to attend, write the time and event in pencil on the monthly calendar and place the invitation in the file marked CALENDAR. Keep your papers filed chronologically by date so you can find them when the day arrives. Also, write yourself a note in your planner to RSVP tomorrow.

FIVE FILE FOLDERS TO HANDLE MAIL

1. CALENDAR
2. HOLDING
3. TO DO
4. TO DECIDE
5. MY INTERESTS

- *Mailers.* These are items such as store announcements, sales, and ads. Decide immediately if these are something that you're going to take advantage of. If so, write them in pencil on your monthly calendar in case you have the time to go to any of the events. Otherwise, throw them away.

- *Schedules.* Take the time to list sports and music events, children's lessons, work, and community events in an abbreviated form in your monthly calendar section in your planner—now. Then file it.

File Folder 2: HOLDING

Place papers in this folder that you are waiting to hear back about, such as something you ordered in a catalog or information related to someone calling you back. On the upper right corner, write the date you called and the approximate date you expect to hear back from someone.

File Folder 3: TO DO

- *Letters.* Enjoy reading them, direct them to other family members, if appropriate, and then mark a "write Aunt Helen back" time on your calendar. Display it or put it in your TO-DO file after marking a calendar date to write back.

- *Catalog ordering.* Determine if you are really going to buy an item from this issue. If so, order immediately and place the order in HOLDING until it arrives. If not, recycle the catalog now.

File Folder 4: TO DECIDE

- *Advertisements.* Keep any sale ad that you think you might take advantage of in this folder. It will be easier to find here than in a stash of papers on the counter. If you are serious about going to this sale, mark your calendar. Keep that one ad in your purse so that you can refer to it.

- *Vacation offers.* Decide if this is a destination or a resort that is worth seriously considering in the near future. If not, don't save it. A travel agent will have plenty of brochures on hand, or you can research the resort on the Internet.

File Folder 5: MY INTERESTS

This is for project ideas, pictures, notes, and sentimental papers that you just like to have around. Be sure to limit this file to no more than half an inch thick.

> *Any time you need to communicate something to someone that they will need to refer back to either for information, affirmation, or comfort, the written word is best. And in these cases, the written word on something tangible like a card or note is the most effective way to communicate.*
> —FLORENCE AND MARITA LITTAUER, *Talking So People Will Listen*

File Drawers

The average household needs two file drawers to handle the necessary papers of life. Some incoming mail that you need to file there would be the following:

- *Mortgage and credit card statements.* Decide what action needs to be taken. Toss any extra advertisements. File any statements under the title of the statement.

- *Bank statements.* Take necessary action, such as balancing the checkbook (at a designated separate time, though), and then file the statement. The most current statements should be at the front of the file.

Bulky Paper Items

Place magazines on a coffee table or magazine holder to go through at your leisure. Maintain a strict system, such as "new one in, old one out," even if you have to read the old one on the spot.

Read and place the daily newspaper on the coffee table for the day. At the earliest possible time in the day, skim the first page of each section before recycling the newspaper with the front page over all the sections.

Determine an area where you will leave mail for the rest of the family. Let them know they have until dinnertime to move it. Don't let their mail pile up on your counter.

Scrutinize your refrigerator door. A clean refrigerator door visually enlarges the size of your kitchen. Of course, refrigerator doors are great places to display the children's artwork or test results, but don't go overboard with clutter. One magnet per child and one paper per magnet.

File the rest of the papers away from the kitchen. Paid bills, receipts, and statements get filed unfolded with the most current paper in the front. If you can keep a year summary page, do so. Then toss the rest.

The Results

It may take a while to perfect this mail system, so don't expect to become letter-perfect the first week you try this. But I guarantee this system works. You're going to love wiping off the mail counter and saying, "I own this space!"

Processing mail is more than just flipping through return address labels. Allow time! Each mail delivery brings an average of fifteen items, so allow a good twenty minutes daily, or two hours weekly, to review and eliminate mail piles. You can lessen the anxiety caused by stacks of paper by tossing 70 percent of your incoming mail after a quick review. You gain 90 percent of the benefit the first time you read a paper, so don't hang on to it to read again "later." Skim it now and let it go.

· ·

What we ever hope to do with ease, we must first learn to do with diligence!
—MOTIVATIONAL POSTER

· ·

Can I Really Simplify My Papers?

Jamie stood in the middle of her kitchen with a wide grin across her face. "Marcia, we did it! No more paper piles, and I know exactly how I am going to get my work done in the future. I finally get it!" I could see the relief in her eyes and the ease in her shoulders.

Jamie is one of hundreds of women whom I have helped transform their avalanche of paper into an organized, efficient paper flow. Whenever I work with a woman and her kitchen papers, I view her paperwork as deserving the same professional treatment that a business president receives in his or her workplace. Every woman deserves to be on top of her paperwork, knowing how to file and retrieve papers and how to get paper-related tasks done quickly. In simplifying your life there is nothing more rewarding than to gain control of your paper piles.

A Paper Philosophy

One of the most important things you can do when you deal with your paper is to listen to what goes on inside your head after you pick it up. For instance, you could adopt the mentality of an organized woman who says something like the following:

> I am in control of my paper. I only keep the papers that I need to actively accomplish things in my life. I do not save it or procrastinate doing it. People with paper piles think, *I'll deal with this later.* But I say, "I am tired of this pile. I am going to get it done now. I own this counter—it doesn't own me."

Begin Today

Starting today, when you enter the kitchen, watch where you put down your mail and purse, and where paper clutter accumulates. Make a concerted effort to deal with and toss those extra papers. And learn to love clean counters! It will give you as much peace of mind as a warm bubble bath that soothes your jangled nerves at the end of a busy day.

The "Get It Done" Paper System Equation
A personal organizing center + a working mail-handling system =
clean counters and no paper piles

The PuSH Sequence for Organizing Paperwork

1. What's the problem?
   - Jamie: Too much paperwork and not enough time.
   - You: _____

2.What's the goal?

- Jamie: Develop systems to organize paper and get work done.
- You: _____

3. What are the time and action steps?

- Jamie: Practice processing daily papers until the pile habit is gone.
- You: _____

4. What's my motivation?

- Jamie: Simplify paperwork and eliminate the stress that paper piles cause.
- You: _____

	P Project	u (You)	S System	H Habit
You	• Conquering paperwork.	• Make a conscious decision of how much paper you will tolerate in your personal space and stick to it.	• Utilize your personal organizing center every day. • Each day starts and ends with a clean counter.	• Make decisions right when you get the mail. • Avoid piles by creating systems that work for you.

Personal Reflection

To see if you are ready to make changes in your current paper-handling system, answer the following questions:

_____ 1. Do you have a pile of papers in your kitchen or on your desk that you should deal with right now?

_____ 2. Do you have more catalogs, magazines, and newspapers than you have time to read and go through?

_____ 3. Are you often frustrated by piles of paper that seem to grow out of control?

_____ 4. Have you ever missed an event because you misplaced the information?

_____ 5. Are you ever embarrassed to invite someone over because of the paper clutter in your home?

_____ 6. Would your life be easier if you improved your paper habits?

A Simple Prayer for Help with Paperwork

Dear God, You see and know my paper problems and the mental peace it robs from my life. It is mounting up, and I need Your help to overcome it.

I praise You that when I ask for wisdom in paperwork—like anything else—You promise to answer. Teach me to decisively deal with my papers until my desk and kitchen counters become a beautiful, enjoyable place reflecting You. Amen.

. . . .

The more organized you are, the fewer piles, files, and crises you will have as you simplify your paperwork.

—MARCIA RAMSLAND, professional organizer

five

Simply Have a Great Day!

Simplifying is a process. It no doubt took you years to build your com-
plicated, high-pressure life. It will take some time to simplify it. You
can't undo it all today. But you can get started today.

—ELAINE ST. JAMES
Living the Simple Life

anessa and Shirley were elementary school teachers attending an organizing workshop that I led recently. I taught a gamut of organizing principles, and everyone had fun seeing the before-and-after pictures of various closets, kitchens, and even garages. The two were thoroughly enjoying themselves, and I could tell they were good friends by the way they elbowed each other and shared a chuckle during my presentation.

As we moved along, I challenged the group by asking them if they knew how long it took them to get ready in the morning and walk out the door. Without looking at each other, Vanessa and Shirley both raised their hands.

"Yup, I know," began Vanessa. "It takes me ten minutes."

"What?" responded Shirley. "You can't possibly get ready in ten minutes. It takes me an hour and fifteen minutes!"

"Sure I can," countered Vanessa. "What takes you so long?"

The pair nearly started arguing, at which point I stepped in and asked if they would hold the details for a moment and look at the big picture instead. "Why do some things take one person so long and others get a lot more done in a day?" I asked. "And why are they both happy with their results?"

What works for one person doesn't necessarily work for someone else. It all depends on the number of people in your house, your routines, and your ability to make changes to shape your day.

But one thing is clear. We all have the ability to control some of our day. The question is, have you ever thought about how to turn your patterns into a better day, or even a great day?

According to my calculations, there are seven elements in each day, which I'll describe in greater detail in just a moment. But for now, just in case your life isn't predictable, you need to have "Plan A" and "Plan B" for days you can't control. This is why I've included a personal time log exercise that will help you assess where your time is going. My goal is for you to lay your head on the pillow each night with a smile, simply having had a great day!

The Seven Elements of a Great Day

A great day is a day where you know where you are going and get the results you want. Sure, there are times when things go awry, and you don't get what you planned. Can you still have a great day? I believe so, especially if you have a skill set waiting in the wings.

To find balance, satisfaction, and a bit of serenity, you need to take a closer look because every day has a pattern to it. These patterns make up what I call the "Seven Elements of a Great Day."

As you read through these seven elements, mark your answers by checking the appropriate boxes and writing in your responses:

1. Preparation

What tasks need to be done the night before to prepare for the next day?
- ❏ Tomorrow's items gathered in one spot
- ❏ Tomorrow's appointments confirmed
- ❏ One last "sweep," putting things away
- ❏ Your habit: _____

2. Start of the Day

How do you start a great day?
- ❏ A hot shower
- ❏ Coffee and the newspaper
- ❏ Exercise
- ❏ Devotions and prayer time
- ❏ A family breakfast
- ❏ Everyone making their own beds and packing their own lunches
- ❏ Your routine: _____

3. Accomplishments

What gets done during a great day?
- ❏ A great proposal written for the boss
- ❏ All the laundry, dishes, and clutter put away
- ❏ A day in the park with your children or grandchildren
- ❏ Time talking with friends
- ❏ A day shaped around whatever needs to be done
- ❏ Your life: _____

4. The People

Who do you like to spend time with during the day? Name them:
- ❏ Family _____
- ❏ Friends _____
- ❏ Coworkers _____
- ❏ New people _____
- ❏ Yourself (doing what?) _____
- ❏ Other: _____

5. Pace

What is the pace of a great day for you?
- ❏ Clipping along at a quick pace

❏ Adrenaline rush from one event to another
❏ Leisurely with no one pressuring me
❏ Inner calm but outer speed
❏ Pondering, reading, and thinking before doing anything
❏ Your favorite pace: _____

6. Spark of Life

What gets you excited during your day?
❏ Shopping!
❏ Stimulating conversation
❏ A new project that I have been put in charge of
❏ Decorating or adding something new to my home
❏ Planning something new in life
❏ Your choice: _____

7. The End

What satisfies you most at the end of the day?
❏ Just making it through
❏ Realizing that I made progress today
❏ Knowing I kept composure in a difficult situation
❏ Having the house clean and ready for tomorrow
❏ Reading to my children as they drifted off to sleep
❏ Your satisfaction: _____

Planning a Great Day Is Like Playing the Piano

I learned the organizing principle of managing my days from playing the piano. When something didn't sound right playing a certain song, I found the page where the problem was and studied it until I found the line of music where I was having problems. Then I was taught to narrow it down to the measure and practice "hands alone" until it was correct. The next step was to practice "hands together" and build it up to tempo, until the whole piece flowed as a harmonious whole. Not only did the piece work better, it sounded better.

A good day is similar. You want to take it apart until you find the problem time slot that keeps tripping you up. Then you can fix it, and your days will start to flow smoothly in ways you enjoy. If you keep looking for your stress points and make the appropriate adjustments, you will find yourself having more great days.

Your Great Day

At this point, think about and even write out what makes a great day for you. Picture yourself living out each of the seven elements as you think it through. Shape each idea until it clearly reflects you. Now you know what you are working toward. Reread what you have written nightly to cast a clear vision for the next day.

Jot It Down

Besides writing out a full description, you can jot down notes in a chart. Personalize this for what you enjoy for a great day. Keep jotting ideas until you come up with something that gives you the big picture of an enjoyable day.

My Great Day Chart

	PREPARA-TION	START	ACCOMP-LISHMENTS	PEOPLE	PACE	SPARK	END
Monday through Friday	Good: Great:	Good: Great:	Good: Great:	Good: Great:	Good: Great:	Good: Great:	Good: Great:
Saturday	Good: Great:	Good: Great:	Good: Great:	Good: Great:	Good: Great:	Good: Great:	Good: Great:
Sunday	Good: Great:	Good: Great:	Good: Great:	Good: Great:	Good: Great:	Good: Great:	Good: Great:

It takes practice to create a string of great days, so even a good day helps toward that goal. Make it a game and keep score for a week if you want! Then simply live it out by being aware of what's happening as you go through your day.

Zero In

I want you to have as many great days as possible. When you are overwhelmed with too many "should's" and "have to's," being aware of your preferences will help you balance everything on your plate and give you a little bit of serenity. If you know what you like, you can reshape the personal parts of your day to become more satisfying.

Controllable and Uncontrollable Days

It's also important to keep in mind two basic elements in every day. You are probably well aware of these two:

- *The controllable part:* These are the events, routines, and transition time you can control. These include your scheduled work hours, preplanned commitments, or anything you agree to put on your calendar.

- *The uncontrollable part:* These are the events beyond your control. These are the things you don't expect or plan for, such as interruptions, crises, illnesses, or emergencies.

Most days will have both elements, and that's a good thing. If we didn't have some unpredictability in our lives, we could become bored with life. So what's the right balance?

Jenny's Story

Jenny sometimes suffers from headaches and migraines that prevent her from getting out of bed. When her migraines develop, she must cancel her plans unexpectedly and stay home. She closes the drapes and does her best to minimize noise until her terrible headaches pass.

We had an appointment to organize her home office one Tuesday morning at ten o'clock. I called her the night before to confirm that everything was lined up, but early the next morning, Jenny phoned me because she had awakened with one of her migraines.

"I just can't make it," Jenny moaned.

"That's okay," I replied. "We can reschedule. Do these migraines happen often?"

"More often than I'd like . . . maybe two or three times a month," Jenny responded.

"In that case, let's not only organize your office but also make a plan for days like this," I said.

"Fine," said Jenny.

Jenny's Solution

Jenny is an example of what it means to have two kinds of days, which is why I offered to help her develop two time strategies. Plan A was for maximizing her "good days," or pain-free days. Plan B was for coping with her "migraine days," when she had no control over what she could accomplish.

Plan A Days: Obviously, on Jenny's good days she could handle her normal life—her home-based business, gym workouts, and volunteer activities at her church.

Plan B Days: When Jenny was feeling subpar, she canceled her appointments, stayed home, and did low-energy, mindless work, like a load of laundry or light magazine reading between bouts of time on the couch. Little got done, but she was okay with that because the migraines laid her low.

Jenny also learned to plan for four days of work at a time. If she was feeling good on the fifth day, then that was a "bonus day," which afforded her extra time. Otherwise if the migraines returned, she went to Plan B, but that was the plan, right?

Plan A and Plan B Days Chart

If you have some days running smoothly, and other days accomplishing little, you might need to plan two kinds of days, such as the women below did.

LIFESTYLES WITH TWO KINDS OF DAYS	PLAN A DAY	PLAN B DAY
Jenny with her migraines	Pain-free day	Pain day
Mother raising kids	Children at school	Children at home
Full-time working woman	Working	Weekends

Postal worker or some-one with shift work	Day shift	Night shift
Woman with a hospitality ministry	Family	Overnight company or dinner guest
Woman volunteering at church or for civic groups	Home day	Day out

Two Kinds of Days to Anticipate

Even though not all of us suffer migraines, we do face two types of days. The first is a 70/30 percent day, when 70 percent is under your control and going smoothly. The other 30 percent is filled with interruptions and unexpected changes you can't control.

The second kind of day is what I call a 30/70 percent day. During this type of day, only 30 percent goes the way you planned, while the other 70 percent turns out to be one of those "just show up for the ride and hang on" days.

Though I have used 70/30 percent in this example, you should decide what percentage applies to you on a majority of days. You may feel like your days are more 80/20, where you can control 80 percent but not the other 20 percent. Whatever the number you come up with, you should focus on what you can control and make it really count.

The key is to focus on the parts of your day you can control, whether it is 70 percent or 30 percent. Some things in life are simply out of your control. Implementing good planning and scheduling will allow you more flexibility for the surprise twists in your day.

. . . .

Remember this about each day: Control the controllable,
and the uncontrollable will take care of itself.

. . . .

Don't allow yourself to get down when something goes wrong or reshapes your day. Just keep going and readjust. You will find it is easier to follow this advice when you are organized and controlling the controllable parts of your life.

168 Hours in Everyone's Week

One easy way to see if you can simplify your days is to determine where your time is going. Each week has 168 hours in it (twenty-four hours times seven days a week). That is all the time you get, whether you are the president of the United States, the mother of five children, or a retiree in a nursing home.

I have used the 168-hours chart successfully for tracking time with students in grade school, high school, and college, and women in all walks of life. That's why I'm confident you can do this on your own.

The funniest result I heard was from Vanessa and Shirley, whom I mentioned at the beginning of the chapter. Shirley took one look at my "168 Hours in My Week" chart and said, "My life won't fit in there."

"That's your problem," laughed Vanessa. "You live as if you can do everything you want to."

With one more elbow jab to each other, they settled down and filled out their charts and chattered away about ways to save time, cut activities, and squeeze in time at the fitness center together. They learned that with a nip here and a tuck there, there were ways they could reshape their lives. You can, too. Let's take a closer look at how.

Track Your Time

1. Use a pencil to block off the following three areas on your 168-hours chart:
   ❏ Sleep
   ❏ Meals and cleanup
   ❏ Your biggest daytime activity, such as caring for and raising children at home or working outside the home

2. After penciling in these three blocked areas, highlight them with three different colors. Have fun and make it colorful.

3. Total the hours spent on each and write the amount in the margin.
   ❏ Sleep = 49 hours (example, seven hours every night)
   ❏ Meals and cleanup = 30 hours (example, 4 hours a day with an extra hour on Saturday and Sunday)
   ❏ Biggest time activity (working outside the home or volunteering at school and church) = 20 to 40 hours

Subtract them from 168 hours in your week. What is left?
_____ hours left

168 HOURS IN MY WEEK

Each time I move something into my time schedule, I have to move
something out. No two things can occupy the same space.

	MON	TUES	WED	THURS	FRI	SAT	SUN
4:00 A.M.			Example: Sleep (7 hours)				
5							
6							
7							
8							
9							
10							
11							
Noon							
1							
2							
3							
4							
5							
6							
7							
8							
9							
10							
11			Example: Sleep (11:00 P.M.–6:00 A.M.)				
Midnight							
1							
2							
3							

4. Group the rest of your time in three other categories, such as these:
   ❏ Transitions = drive time, kids coming home
   ❏ Family/TV/computer time = evenings, weekends
   ❏ Classes or meetings = events that require your time
   Subtract them from 168 hours in your week. What is left?

   _____ hours left

What Is Normal?

Most women, at this point, have ten to twenty hours of free time left over. This is good! If you have no free time left over, then you are living one high-strung, fast-paced life. Something's got to give, and I hope it won't be you.

On the other hand, if you have more than twenty hours of free time in a week, you could be bored or missing your purpose in life. You may need to add a few more social events at this point.

Either way, you can simplify your life by taking stock of where your time is really going. Is your schedule bringing you the results you want? Of course, you have to reserve a couple of hours as free time. After you've done that and recognize you are overscheduled or underscheduled, you can make changes. You now have the opportunity to balance your days.

Make Every Day Count

Your time should reflect your personal priorities so that you can accomplish what is most important in your life at this time. Your calendar and 168-hours chart are reflections of who you are and what you want to accomplish in life.

Likes and Dislikes

To really evaluate where you are, make two columns titled "Things I Like about My Life Right Now" and "Things I Don't Like about My Life." Take five minutes to list everything (here or in a notebook) that comes to mind. Total each column.

Likes   Dislikes

_____   _____

_____   _____

_____   _____

_____   _____

_____   _____

Once you review your lists, look to see if you can change anything in the "Dislikes" column that would enable you to move it over to the "Likes" column. If you don't like housework, you might save up for a part-time cleaning lady. If you don't like paperwork, you might swap baby-sitting time with a friend who does.

For most women, a great day is not just full of activities they enjoy, but it is also filled with quieter things as well. For instance Kathy, a mother of two children and a women's speaker, said a great day is getting a task accomplished and having some quiet time each day at home when everyone else is gone.

For Cindi, a women's ministry director, having a great day meant checking off several things from her to-do list and making a difference in the lives of people she loves by keeping in touch by phone each week.

And for B. J., a creative arts director who works with several choirs and a drama group, a great day is feeling connected to God and inspired in her work to create a new presentation for the next Sunday's service.

What makes a great day is up to you. Be aware of what brings out the best in you and gives you confidence to get through the day. Glance in the mirror as you pass by and say, "What can I change to make this a great day?" Smile . . . and then do it.

Ten Dos and Don'ts to Simplify Your Day

Dos	Don'ts
1. Do stay ahead of the game by arriving early and finishing things ahead of time.	1. Don't leave home late and have to be in a rush to make all your appointments.
2. Do limit your multitasking to no more than three things and wrap them up as you go along.	2. Don't multitask yourself into fragmentation with undone chores trailing behind you.
3. Do look for emotional rest spots and space them throughout your day to renew your attitude.	3. Don't drive yourself (and others) into frustration by tackling too many problems at once.
4. Do look people in the eye and "be present."	4. Don't overlook the person in front of you to accomplish your agenda.
5. Do know what you're having for dinner and when you're starting it.	5. Don't forget dinner is coming and scramble at the last minute.

6. Do "time slot" everything into the day, especially things you really want to do.	6. Don't expect everything will get done just because it's on your list.
7. Do be realistic about what you can accomplish today based on yesterday's success.	7. Don't keep everything in front of you, but just things you plan to accomplish today.
8. Do start doing things as soon as possible so you can enjoy your progress.	8. Don't put things off until you're good and ready, or they might not happen.
9. Do something you enjoy every day— call a friend, read a book, or take a walk.	9. Don't push yourself so hard that you lose your pleasant personality.
10. Do keep working at a knotty time problem until you hit upon a solution.	10. Don't accept frustrations in your day as a permanent part of your life.

Personal Reflection

The best way to have a great day is to know where your time is going and make changes from there.

You might prefer your daily pace to be leisurely with no pressure, which is fine. On the other hand, your days may turn out to be jam-packed without a moment to rest. That's okay. You can learn from today and make a better plan for tomorrow. Always keep improving and simplify your days to be focused on what matters to you. You can control your days more than you think you can.

1. I think I use my time best when _____.

2. I regret that lately I have not had the time to _____.

3. If someone gave me an extra hour just for myself each week, I would

_____.

4. The two people I would like to spend more time with would be

_____ and _____.

5. When I retire, I plan to _____.

A Simple Prayer for Better Days

Dear God, thank You for each day. I'm sorry I complain so much. I really have it quite good. Instead of asking You for more time, could You please help me plan my days better? I will try to believe that there is enough time in each day to accomplish all that I really need to do. Help me to take steps to simply have more great days. Amen.

. . . .

Time is like money—
the less you have
the more carefully you need to spend it.

—Marcia Ramsland, professional organizer

section two

Simplify Your Systems

Streamline your daily systems at home . . .

- The First System: Maximize Mealtimes
- The Second System: Lighten Up Laundry and Closets
- The Third System: Conquer Cleaning and Clutter
- The Fourth System: Power Through Projects

six

The First System: Maximize Mealtimes

A simple menu, laughter and love are all ingredients you need for a memorable meal.

—ANN MATTURRO
writer

Sharon came floating into the house bubbling over with happiness. During an important project meeting earlier that day, everyone had applauded for all that she accomplished the last six months. She hadn't received so many accolades in years, and it felt good. *I think they really appreciate me, and even my boss was impressed. It was worth all the hard work!* she thought.

But as she entered the kitchen, her face fell. Sharon paused with the day's packages and papers in hand. *Why am I so productive at work but always feel so let down when I have to come home and cook?* The busy working mother resisted the urge to turn around and buy fast food for dinner. Instead, she picked up the phone and called me.

"Marcia, you helped me get organized at my office," she said. "Is there any way I can simplify the dinnertime chaos at home? I've only got thirty minutes until we eat."

I assured her that I could help her simplify her kitchen and mealtimes, but I needed more than the next thirty minutes. "You must be doing something right because your family is eating every day," I said teasingly.

Sharon laughed. "Yes, they look well fed as a matter of fact. But it's me that needs help. Lately, my biggest pressures of the day revolve around dinnertime, and I don't know why."

"Well, here's what we can do for tonight," I said. "Just get through dinner, and then give me a call. We can talk about four key elements that can simplify meals. It's not as hard as you think."

Meals, the Premier System

Every day millions of women like Sharon share one common household task—dealing with the age-old refrain known as "What's for dinner?" While some women prefer to do laundry and cleaning, they understand that preparing meals ranks at the top in keeping family life running smoothly. You can skip a day of laundry or postpone some house cleaning, but you can't neglect feeding the family. That's why developing a meal system that works every day is so important for everyone concerned, including yourself.

Mealtimes are important because your children and husband are hungry, and they're looking forward to eating something delicious and satisfying—and good health depends on eating nutritious food. Family meals also provide a respite from the day's activities. But as we all know, cooking can be time-consuming and stressful, unless you have a good system in place.

Maximize Mealtimes

Sharon made sloppy joes and salad for her family that night. "I got through that dinner," she said, "but I am fresh out of ideas. What are the four systems for meals?"

"Without realizing it, you are already taking care of all the components," I replied. "But if you can identify where your strengths and weaknesses are, you can get the whole dinnertime process going more smoothly." I then outlined the four elements:

- Simple menu planning
- Timesaving cleanup
- An organized kitchen setup
- Streamlined grocery shopping

"The goal," as I explained it to Sharon, "is to simplify dinnertimes so that we can enjoy family time around meals and maintain a beautiful kitchen without much fuss."

Jump-Start Your Menus

Let's face it, many women procrastinate thinking about dinner until the last minute and then pull together one of the old standards like macaroni-and-cheese, hamburgers, or spaghetti. In fact, studies show women get caught in a rut cooking the same three to five meals over and over. The actual cooking isn't that difficult; it's deciding *what* to make that is.

TIMESAVING ELEMENTS FOR MEALTIMES

- Simple menu planning
- Timesaving cleanup
- An organized kitchen
- Streamlined grocery shopping

Sharon, too, began thinking about dinner at 5 P.M., which often limited her options. She knew that home-cooked meals offered better nutrition than a quick swing through the McDonald's drive-through lane or a delivered pizza. She also knew that good ol' home cooking also costs a lot less than eating out. But knowing it and doing it were difficult with the time pressures that were mounting in her life.

Fourteen Meals That Save the Day

To solve the problem of a limited menu plan, I invited Sharon to take a pad of paper and pen to the dinner table and ask her family what they would like to eat. "Tell them you need to make a list of fourteen meals," I said. "Ask them simply, 'What would you like to eat for dinner?'"

The next night the family joined in, and soon they came up with a list of great meal ideas, many that she had forgotten about. Afterward, Sharon posted the list inside a kitchen cabinet for instant menu ideas and to help her shop for the right ingredients. Sharon felt much better, and the family was excited that some of their favorite meals would be served in the near future.

How Long Does It Take?

I suggested that Sharon identify the amount of time spent on a meal from the minute she walked into the kitchen until cleanup was complete. Sharon noticed that dinner preparation was often interrupted by phone calls, returning voice messages, the kids asking questions about homework, and sorting through the mail. All these tasks, including meal preparation to clean up, often kept her in the kitchen from 5 until 8 or 9 P.M.

When she added almost an hour in the kitchen each morning to serve breakfast, make school lunches, and clean up, she was easily spending five hours a day on meal-related tasks. The weekends were even longer since the family often ate lunch together. Sharon figured she was averaging almost six hours a day in the kitchen, or one-third of her waking hours, on average, each day!

Sharon was surprised at how much time was frittered away in the kitchen. It's not that she minded kitchen duty, but she felt her time was being spent too haphazardly with less-than-satisfying results. She was motivated to make changes, so we developed a sample two-week menu plan to jump-start her dinner planning. We even included estimated preparation times to help her plan better.

Sharon's Two-Week Master Menu Plan

SUNDAY	MONDAY	TUESDAY	WEDNESDAY	THURSDAY	FRIDAY	SATURDAY
90 min. (Company) Roast Beef Mashed Potatoes Salad Bread Lemon Cake	30 min. Spaghetti Tossed Salad French Bread Ice Cream	20 min. Tuna Melts Carrot Sticks Watermelon (Kids' Sports Night)	40 min. Baked Chicken Rice Broccoli-Cauliflower Mix Frozen Yogurt	30 min. Creamy Chicken Casserole with Rice Tossed Salad Dinner Rolls	60 min. Lasagna Tossed Salad Garlic Bread Ice Cream	40 min. Grilled Salmon Brown Rice French-Style Green Beans Apple Pie
30 min. Grilled Steaks Baked Potatoes Corn on the Cob Fresh Fruit	30 min. Lemon Grilled Chicken Rice Tossed Salad	20 min. Sloppy Joes French Fries Fruit Salad Brownies	30 min. Chicken Oriental Casserole Peas (Music Recital)	45 min. Ham Baked Beans Coleslaw Ice Cream	30 min. Chili Tossed Salad Bread Pie (Johnsons for Dinner)	45 min. Grilled Pork Chops Applesauce Rolls Pudding

As she tried out her written menus, Sharon became more realistic by substituting some easier menus for the more ambitious ones. She learned to watch her calendar for evening activities and plan a simpler meal on those nights. The "special" meals were earmarked for weekends or when company was invited over.

Quick Menu Tips

- Post your family's "14 Favorite Meals" list inside your kitchen cabinet for quick reference.

- Jot down your meals for the week ahead.

- Think about what you're going to cook for dinner in the morning and check to see if the necessary ingredients are on hand.

- Teach your children to help in the kitchen by showing them how to shred lettuce, dice tomatoes, and chop carrot sticks.

- Let your husband take over some of the kitchen territory, too, since more men nowadays are enjoying time in the kitchen.

- Use a calendar in the kitchen just to record meals. This will provide a sense of accomplishment and help you plan ahead.

....

Encouraging good eating habits in children must start with a daily family effort.

—Dr. Christine Wood, *How to Get Kids to Eat Great and Love It!*

....

Timesaving Tips for Kitchen Cleanup

Next, Sharon and I addressed cleanup and her lack of motivation getting the dishes into the dishwasher and putting all the pots and pans away. "Sometimes I don't get to the dishes until 10 P.M.," Sharon confided. "I am just too tired after dinner to actually clean up. When that happens, I've even let the dirty dishes stack up for several days. And then it's really a pain to get the dishes clean."

"You're right," I said. "Just because you're done eating doesn't mean you're finished with dinner. Use some of the momentum from a good conversation and great food to carry you through the cleanup process. All it takes is about fifteen minutes of concentrated effort, and you're finished," I replied.

Five Steps for a 15-Minute Meal Cleanup

Cleanup can be done faster than you think.

1. Clear the table and leave only the centerpiece. Load the dishwasher, collect hand-wash items, and put the leftovers away ASAP. Get the whole family involved to speed up the process. (Time: five minutes)
2. Set up a rotating family schedule for dish washing. Wash the remaining pots and pans right after the meal before they get crusty and take twice as long to get done. (Time: five minutes)
3. Wipe off the table and the kitchen counters. (Time: one minute)
4. Put the dried dishes and the drying rack away as soon as possible. A kitchen always looks messy if dishes are continually drying on the counter. (Time: two minutes)
5. Empty the garbage and clean the floor as needed. (Time: two minutes)

Total time spent in cleanup: fifteen minutes. Now you're finished for the evening and can do something else you enjoy!

Sharon learned to enjoy cleanup almost as much as her accomplishments at work. She recognized that the kitchen was the hub of family life and worth the effort to maintain. She even decided to purchase a new silk-flower centerpiece for the kitchen table—the center of most good conversations in a home.

Now her kitchen looked like a showcase model home, clean and organized, and all she did was improve her menu planning and clean up right after each meal. She was happier, but we were not finished yet.

Simplify for a Beautiful Kitchen

The third system I walked Sharon through was to simplify the kitchen itself. Countertop clutter can drive any woman crazy at dinnertime. Like Sharon, stop now and survey your kitchen like an impartial observer. Is there anything that could be put away to give your kitchen a clutter-free makeover?

Clutter has a way of creeping into the kitchen each day until the countertops are covered with "stuff" that needs to be dealt with or thrown away. Too much stuff, even if it is organized and practical, distracts from the simplicity and beauty of the most-used room in the house—the kitchen. The front two-thirds of any counter should be clear, and the back one-third should have only useful and attractive things on it.

Kitchen Clutter Cleanup

After Sharon cleaned up the dishes the next evening, I urged her to simplify her kitchen counters. In just a short amount of time, she was able to shape up her kitchen by following these steps:

- Pull things forward on the counters, then wash each item and the countertop. Find "homes" out of sight for as many items as possible.

- Place larger appliances in corner spaces and store less-used appliances in cabinets. Again, keep the front two-thirds of each counter empty.

- Keep attractive, useful items on display and recycle excess knickknacks. Display only what you like and regularly use.

Remember: Countertop clutter is never stylish, so be ruthless and make sure everything gets put away. Guard your clean counters like the beefeaters at Buckingham Palace!

Sharon found plastic bags stuffed between canisters, chipped knickknacks wedged between cookbooks, some loose board-game pieces and CDs floating around, and old grocery flyers waiting for the recycle bin. After she put everything away and hung some matching dishtowels, the kitchen looked much better and even felt inviting.

Groaning or Growing with Grocery Savvy

The fourth and final system I discussed with Sharon was simplifying the grocery shopping. She told me that this was an area where she knew she was wasting time and money. She said she was ready to get more organized to save time, money, and stress.

I encouraged her not to think of finding the perfect system of trying to nail down every bargain out there. Then we shared ways that she could streamline the process. Here's what we came up with:

- Put a magnetic grocery list and pen on the refrigerator to list items when you run out of them. Teach your family to write down what they would like you to buy at the supermarket.

- Make a grocery list consisting of ingredients for five dinner menus and plan the other two meals based on available store specials.

- Save money by challenging yourself to see how closely you can stick to your original grocery list.

- Get a coupon holder you like and selectively clip coupons only for what you regularly use.

- Resolve to get in and get out of the supermarket as quickly as possible. No loitering.

Studies show if you enter a supermarket with a list in hand and get your shopping done in less than forty-five minutes, you save the most money. For every five minutes after that, you spend an extra ten dollars. The least expensive food budget includes two pick-ups per week. That means one major shopping trip plus one quick pick-up for fresh items.

Sharon learned to avoid the dinner rush hour at the grocery store by going earlier in the week and on the way home from meetings. That saved time since the aisles weren't jammed and the checkout lines were uncrowded. "I always knew this, but I didn't realize I had fallen into the 'dinner rush hour' at the supermarket again," she said.

As for her refrigerator list, another big help happened when Sharon's girlfriend Mary Beth produced a sample grocery list by sections in the store. Sharon placed this list on her refrigerator door and wrote in items that she needed to buy on her next shopping trip. This is what her simple list looked like:

Sample Grocery List by Store Sections

Fresh Produce:	Meat:
Deli:	Canned and Packaged Goods:
Bakery:	Frozen Foods:
Dairy:	Household Items:

Writing a grocery list by shopping categories saved time at the store just by organizing the list at home. Another option would be to create a computer printout of your most-used grocery items. Circle the items needed during your next grocery run, and keep extra copies on hand.

Expert Level

- Menus: Challenge yourself to see how many nights you can go without repeating the same meal. Try creating a meal plan for an entire month.

- Menus: Sort, organize, and clean up your recipe box or files to look attractive. Incorporate the saved "to try" recipes once a week.

- The kitchen: Match your utensils and decorations to your favorite color scheme.

- The kitchen: Get rid of cooking items you no longer use, and upgrade old utensils as a personal perk for all the meals you cook.

- Cleanup: Work toward a dishless sink and spotless counters as you get better and better.

Problem-Solving Dinner Schedules

"This is great, but I have one more question," chirped Sharon. "It never seems we can sit down together because of sports, meetings, and unpredictable workdays. What can we do about that?"

"We faced that problem at our house, too," I replied. "Mark, my teenage son, said, 'Mom, it would really help if we ate before Dad got home. I'm always late for things after supper, and it's embarrassing.'" Mark often had to run to a basketball game, a Bible study, or a youth group meeting.

Since Mark had very few requests, I thought we should address this. Was there a way we could eat together and he could get to his games and meetings on time?

My solution was to eat with Mark at 5:30 P.M. and sit down with my husband at 6:30, which is usually when he arrived home from work. On evenings when I had something going on, Mark and I would eat a half-hour earlier at five. That way I had enough time to get the dishes done before I left, and I didn't come home to a kitchen that needed clean up at 10:00 P.M.

I learned that the busier our family was, the more I needed to plan meals to get us together. Since we were all busy during the week, we made it a high priority to sit down to eat together on the weekends. We made Friday night a special dinner night to celebrate finishing the week well. With three people on very different schedules, it didn't hurt to double-check with them at breakfast about their evening plans and readjust dinner accordingly. It seemed easier when all three of our children were younger and I could control the family schedule for the five of us.

Sharon agreed that it was worth figuring out the best dinnertime for her family each night. She began by jotting another note on her menu calendar:

Normal dinnertime: 6:00 P.M.

Early dinner: 5:30 P.M.

By adding the preparation time to each menu, she could more accurately get dinner on the table at the time she planned. "Now if I can quit answering the phone, doing homework with the kids, and glancing through the mail, this should work," she laughed.

That's right. If you multitask without keeping an eye on the clock, dinner preparation will be chaotic and lengthy. Become aware of what works best for your family schedule a week at a time. This is one system that is well worth simplifying in life.

TEN TIMESAVING TIPS FOR MEALS

1. Begin with a clean kitchen.
2. Make sure the clean dishes are out of the dishwasher.
3. Set the table before cooking to motivate yourself to get dinner going.
4. Estimate how long it will take to get a meal ready, and then try to beat the clock.
5. Prepare the longest part of the meal first.
6. Decide what can be done while another dish is baking.
7. Avoid traffic jams at the kitchen sink by keeping your wastebasket out while cooking.
8. Place a stool nearby so the kids and guests can talk while dinner is being made.
9. Alert everyone five minutes before a meal so you can sit down together.
10. Remember, a good meal is more than the food. It's also about the mood, so be cheerful when you sit down together.

Did You Know?

For a final tidbit of information I asked Sharon, "Do you know when the most arguments occur in a family?"

"I'm not sure," she replied.

"Well, studies show that most arguments happen the half-hour before meals."

"No wonder I was in a rut at dinnertimes!" she exclaimed. "I didn't have anything ready, and everyone got cranky."

From then on, Sharon's dinners were prepared on time, and the family actually looked forward to eating and talking together.

Personal Reflection

As you can surmise, the further ahead you plan for mealtimes and the more you streamline your kitchen systems, the more time you will have to put into other equally worthwhile areas of your life. Spend your time with family and friends at dinner, not bogged down in preparation and cleanup.

Ask yourself these questions to see where you are right now:

_____ 1. Am I in a "menu rut" cooking the same three to five meals over and over?

_____ 2. Are mealtimes something to look forward to at my house?

_____ 3. Is there something I could do to streamline my systems and maximize mealtime conversations?

_____ 4. Is there someone who needs my friendship over a home-cooked meal?

With all the meals ahead of us as women, it is important to remember the brighter side of dinnertime. Sure, try new recipes, but also vary your menus, speed up cleanup, and improve how you keep your kitchen counters clean. Make meals an easier task from start to finish. When that happens, invite some friends over and enjoy their company to reward your lifestyle change.

If you are organized and prepared, dinnertime will become more of a joy and less of a chore. You can do it. *Bon appétit!*

A Simple Prayer of Thanks

Dear God, thank You for the blessings of family and friends. Help my kitchen to become a place of refuge from the day and encouragement for facing whatever life brings tomorrow. Fill our mealtimes with love and laughter. And help me to make changes that will make it fun to be at my house. Amen.

. . . .

Hospitality, like charity, must begin at home. . . . How we all long to hear, "It's so good to have you home," or those other words, "It's so good to come home to you."

—KAREN MAINS, *Open Heart, Open Home*

seven

The Second System:
Lighten Up Laundry and Closets

I've discovered that I can save energy by sorting the laundry while the piles are small and manageable. I also put the piles in the order of the ages of family members. Then I don't have to figure where each pile is.

—SANDRA FELTON
The New Messies Manual

One Monday, Katie waved her kids off to school and walked into the house through the back door. She nearly tripped over a pile of dirty towels and muttered to herself, "Seems like these piles just grow when I'm not looking. Didn't I just do the laundry on Friday?"

Being an energetic woman, she tossed the towels into the washing machine and decided to sort the rest of the baskets right then. As she pulled apart the last overflowing pile, she stopped in midair. *How come this laundry never gets done? I may end up spending every morning for the rest of my life doing this,* she thought.

Across town, I was organizing her mother's closet. Myrna had a closet full of nice clothes, but it needed to be organized and thinned out. We worked steadily to organize the hanging clothes, line up shoes and purses, refold sweaters and tops, and create a large pile of giveaway items that Myrna no longer liked or used. By noon, we were almost finished when Katie called.

"Mom, I've got to pick up Emily from the kindergarten bus, and I only got a couple loads of wash done. Isn't there a better way?"

Myrna invited me in on the phone call, and we agreed that they were each dealing with two ends of the same time-consuming spectrum—keeping up with clothes. Managing a wardrobe makes laundry and organizing closets go hand in hand. The challenge is to find better ways to simplify both systems until they work for you, instead of you for them.

Tackling the Laundry

I assured Katie that laundry piles could be managed and needn't fill her days or take over her life. I also redirected her sights by describing how satisfying it would be to wake up with all the clothes neatly hanging in the closet and folded in the drawers. "It's amazing how much easier mornings will go when the family doesn't have to hunt around for the clothes they want to wear," I said. "Everything they want is where it should be and ready to go."

Same-Day Laundry Principle

As Katie and Myrna continued to listen on the phone, I shared my story that led to my "same-day laundry principle."

One summer I was teaching a five-part class about getting organized. After I had given classes on the principles and systems of successful meals and cleaning, the women told me how delighted they were with the changes they were making at home.

Feeling confident because of their enthusiastic responses, I launched into explaining the next system, doing laundry. Instantly, the mood in the room changed. I saw thirty women fold their arms and roll their eyes.

I learned a valuable lesson that day: Women will let you teach them anything, except how to do their laundry. They believe they have a good system just because they are multi-tasking while the washing machine is going. That's not necessarily true.

Instead of further instruction on a "right" way to do laundry, however, I challenged the class to consider their existing laundry system against the following principle: You have a successful laundry system if the clothes that go in the washing machine complete the four steps of washing, drying, folding, and being put away—in the same day!

At this point, all the women laughed because they had at least one laundry basket full of clean clothes waiting to be put away, or still sitting in the dryer. But to their credit, they were open to hearing me describe why my same-day laundry principle was the best way to go.

"SAME DAY" LAUNDRY PRINCIPLE

You have a successful laundry system if the clothes that go in the washing machine complete the four steps of washing, drying, folding, and being put away—in the same day!

| Wash | + | Dry | + | Fold | + | Put Away | = | Success! |

When I described my same-day principle to Katie, she wanted to know more about how to actually accomplish that goal. With pens in hand, we began to strategize right over the phone.

Save Time before You Start

Our first step was to determine the number of loads that needed to be done. We took this amount and planned it over the whole week. Our goal was to avoid the overwhelming amount of laundry that Katie faced each Monday morning.

Katie thought she had seven loads of wash each week for her family. The breakdown went like this:

- Whites (two loads)
- Darks (one load)
- Towels (two loads)
- Bed linens (two loads)

Katie was home during the week, but she was very busy on the weekends with the kids' sports and running errands with her husband. So we arranged her laundry schedule for Monday through Friday, leaving the weekend to spend with her family instead of her wash.

Stay-at-Home Mom with Seven Loads of Laundry
(Wash from Monday through Friday.)

MONDAY	TUESDAY	WEDNESDAY	THURSDAY	FRIDAY	SATURDAY	SUNDAY
two loads: whites, towels	two loads: darks, sheets— parents and daughter	X	one load: sheets from both sons	two loads: whites, towels	X	X

"But I am thinking about going back to work soon," Katie said. "I worry if I set up a schedule like this, it will all have to change when I go to work, and then I will have to spend my entire weekend doing wash." To allay her fears about being a working mom and never catching up, we made out another schedule.

Working Mom with Seven Loads of Laundry
(Wash in the evenings and on Saturdays.)

MONDAY	TUESDAY	WEDNESDAY	THURSDAY	FRIDAY	SATURDAY	SUNDAY
two loads: whites, towels	X	X	two loads: whites, darks	X	three loads: towels and two loads of sheets	X

Instead of doing all seven loads on Saturday and Sunday, Katie could see how she could spread out the loads during the week and still be done by noon on Saturday. If an evening event came up, all she had to do was rotate the wash to the day before or after the scheduled day.

No longer would Katie have to feel defeated or surprised about finding wet towels in the washing machine. She now had a system, and she could control it. With a laundry schedule posted on three-by-five cards in the laundry room and beside the clothes hampers, she could remind the family the day before of what was getting washed and look forward to getting it out of the way.

Katie put a clock on the wall above the washer and dryer and also used a kitchen timer to remind her when to move the load. She allowed thirty minutes for washing, thirty minutes for the dryer, and thirty minutes for folding and putting it away. It became easier to figure out how much time in a day her wash would take:

one load = 1.5 hours
two loads = two hours*
three loads = 2.5 hours*

* By adding a load of wash every time one went to the dryer, it only added a half-hour each time.

Ten Timesaving Laundry Tips

While laundry will be an ongoing part of life, it doesn't have to be never ending. Here are some tips to stay on track through the most difficult parts: sorting and putting away.

1. Place a wall clock above the washer and dryer.
2. Be ready to move clothes to the next step after thirty minutes.
3. Wash those items first that require the most sorting afterward.
4. Minimize wrinkles by immediately folding warm clothes from the dryer.
5. Save time by making the bed with the sheets straight from the dryer.
6. Stack clean towels by bathrooms to speed up delivery.
7. Leave the washer lid open as a signal to empty the dryer.
8. Save steps by keeping a lint box or wastebasket nearby.
9. Hang the empty laundry basket on a hook.
10. Close the lid after your last load and congratulate yourself for finishing all your laundry for the day!

Decorate your laundry room to be a pleasant place. A pretty wall hanging, some paint, a mirror, or even a family vacation photo will brighten your day as you wash and put away clothes.

Minimal Laundry Needs

Myrna had been listening patiently to my conversation with her daughter, but she and her husband had very little wash to do. "Laundry isn't a problem for me," she said afterward, "but is there something I should know?"

With such a light schedule, I told her, it wasn't necessary to assign days, but it would be helpful to figure out a way to minimize washing everything each week. I suggested listing what she needed and then operating on a rotating A and B week schedule.

I pointed out that Myrna and Katie could save twenty-five loads of wash in a year if they washed some loads only every other week. For example, they could purchase enough white underwear, socks, and T-shirts and wash them every other week. Here is a sample chart:

> **A and B Weeks for Fewer Loads of Wash**
> A Week: Two loads, plus hand wash = whites, darks, and hand wash.
> B Week: Three loads, plus ironing = towels, sheets, shirts, and ironing.

For both ladies, writing and posting the schedule on three-by-five cards by the washing machine (and the clothes hamper) simplified their lives. For the first time in a long while, Myrna and Katie felt in control of how much time they spent on laundry.

Ironing or Wrinkles?

For those who iron, like Myrna and sometimes Katie, there are two different philosophies at work:

- Ironing weekly. Some people like to do all of their ironing at one time. This is a good method if you have enough clothes for a week for yourself and family members. You can also iron while watching TV or catching up on phone calls.

- Ironing daily. For those who prefer to iron each day, try not to keep the ironing board set up all the time. An ironing board can be a huge clutter item that detracts from a peaceful home.

Katie found she could also minimize her ironing if she purchased clothes with a small percentage of synthetic content. This meant that they looked fresher without ironing.

Organizing Closets

By midafternoon, Myrna and I had finished organizing her walk-in closet. When we were finished, she couldn't contain herself any longer. She had to call her daughter.

"Katie, you have to come over and see my closet," she said. "You won't believe it. It's so organized that it looks like Nordstrom's!"

Katie and little Emily came right over, and we gave them a tour of the "cleanest walk-in closet in the neighborhood." Their eyes lit up as they congratulated Myrna on her beautiful closet. Naturally, Katie wondered how we did it, so I shared the three-step process with her:

Step 1: Organize and Simplify Hanging Clothes

For a fresh closet makeover, Myrna and I worked from left to right on the hanging rod, organizing a section at a time. Sometimes it was easier to pull a whole section out and rehang items in the right category; other times there was enough room to just move the hangers into the right spot. We spent the most time placing the jackets, blouses, and slacks in their own categories and from dark to light colors. Myrna used matching hangers to give everything a clean, crisp look, including spacing the hangers one-half to one inch apart.

"But then we did the best part," Myrna told her daughter. "We counted and wrote down the number of blouses, slacks, and dresses I owned. Wow! I had a lot more than I thought. When I divided the total number of dresses by the estimated number of times I wore them, I realized I had way too many."

"So what did you do about it?" Katie asked.

"We pulled out each hanger and asked, 'Do I like this, and do I still want to wear it?' That made it easy to put things in a giveaway pile right next to a dry-clean pile and a to-fix pile. I feel so relieved to have all my favorites in my closet where I can find them and the so-so items being passed to someone else who can use them."

Katie was impressed at her mother's organized and simplified closet, and even little Emily clapped with glee before she sat down on the clean floor. "Look, Grandma, I can play here!"

Step 2: Vacuum the Floor and Organize Shoes

Myrna continued. "After we did all the hanging clothes, we pulled out everything on the floor and vacuumed thoroughly. Oh, the dust! I even found a pair of my favorite shoes that I had been looking for."

By lining up all the shoes from dressy to casual and from dark to light, Myrna could see what she had. We revived a discarded shoe rack until she could shop for a contemporary shoe holder that would be convenient to slip her shoes into.

From the floor we discarded forgotten bags of items and old purses. We gathered up sewing materials and placed them elsewhere in the house. We even found a few forgotten Christmas gifts. I reminded Myrna that her closet was for clothes and dressing each day, not a storage catchall.

Step 3: Refold and Simplify Shelving Items

After sorting the hanging clothes and the closet floor, Myrna knew what she had, which made it easier to decide what to keep on her shelving. She pulled sweaters, T-shirts, and athletic wear down, cleaned the shelves with soapy water, and pondered what to keep and what could go.

"Go back to our two rules," I said, as I repeated them for her:

- Keep only what you like and use.
- Keep clothes that reflect your current lifestyle.

When Myrna looked at her large collection of hats and visors that matched her tennis outfits, she sighed and dropped them in the giveaway bag. "With my arthritis, I guess my tennis days are over. But that's okay, I have enough clothes to go out to lunch with my girlfriends instead."

On the shelves we arranged her current purses from dark to light, and we refolded sweaters so that one rounded "decorative edge" faced smoothly forward. Sportswear and lounging clothes were placed according to frequency of use. We used lower shelving if those clothes were worn each week or drawers if there wasn't enough rod space. Less-used items were stored on the highest shelf in labeled boxes.

The Best Day to Clean Closets

There is one day that is the best to weed out the family clothes closets. Do you know what that day is? Katie was amazed to hear me tell her that it is laundry day—because everything the family likes is in the washing machine, and the least-favorite items are still in the closet. Those are the clothes you want to scrutinize and consider giving away.

If you haven't worn something in the past six months, consider giving it to a friend or charity. People in your community and around the world need clothes, so make someone happy while gaining some valuable space in your closet. You can also receive a tax deduction for giving clothes to charity. Be sure to keep a list for your records.

After weeding out your clothes, it's time to organize your closet. For an organized look, get matching hangers, and always place the empty ones at one end of the rod. Now make sure all the items are laundered and in the closet. That way everything is there, and you can start simplifying the closet contents.

Remember, most people wear 20 percent of their total wardrobe 80 percent of the time. Get rid of the unworn 80 percent excess by passing it on to someone who can use it. An organized closet is priceless for creating a stress-free environment each morning.

Establish an in-and-out rule. Every time a new item comes into the house, show an old item the door.

KATHY PEEL, family manager

Expert Challenge Level

- In deep drawers, "stairstep" stacking items, like T-shirts or pants, so you can see one inch of every item from top to bottom. Use shoeboxes or plastic containers in drawers to hold small items in place.

- Get a picture from a magazine or catalog and fold your clothes the same appealing way. Each stacked item should have the smooth "decorative edge" showing, with multiple edges from sleeves in sweaters or the edges of towels toward the back.

- Keep a numbered inventory of items in each category (such as tops, slacks, sweaters, nylons, and jackets). If you don't have to wear the same thing twice in the next three weeks, you probably have enough clothes.

- Minimize sorting time by putting a hamper, lightweight basket, or laundry bag in each bedroom closet. You can fill up their load of whites by washing their bedsheets at the same time.

THREE-STEP CLOSET ORGANIZING

You will enjoy waking up to an organized closet after you clean thoroughly. Keep—and wear—your favorite things that make you feel good. Pass on things you don't like or use.

1. Group hanging items by category and put unused items in a donation bag.
2. Empty, vacuum, and neatly return the floor items.
3. Clean off the shelves and put back only what you like and use.

The Fabulous 52-Week Simplifying Technique

Myrna and Katie realized there was more to organizing clothes than just dealing with the closet. Katie wondered how she could organize her bathroom cabinet, which was filled with her makeup, shampoo bottles, and zillions of hair things for Emily. "It seems like I'm always in a rush when I need to find something, and then I never have time to organize them," said Katie.

"'The fabulous 52-week simplifying technique' is the secret for busy people," I replied. "I heard about this from one of my audience participants, who had to be the busiest, yet most put-together working mom I have ever seen. She said the secret to staying organized was to clean out one drawer or shelf every Sunday night, which was the only uncommitted time she had as a single mom. This helped her stay ahead of the clutter in her home and gave her a sense of order at the start of the week."

If you clean out one drawer every week, you can simplify everything relating to clothes, laundry, and getting dressed. Following is a more detailed explanation of how it works.

The Next Ten Things to Simplify

Find a calendar just for your dressing area where you can keep a ten-item list going. Resolve to accomplish one simplifying project a week, such as Friday morning, Saturday morning, or Sunday night. Here are ten examples for your personalized fabulous 52-week simplifying list:

1. Organize your jewelry drawer (earrings, necklaces, and bracelets).
2. Simplify and clean items in your makeup drawer.
3. Organize and toss extra items under the bathroom sinks, such as unused shampoos and cleaning supplies.
4. Refold your sweaters and tops on the shelves.
5. Sort and match your belts with your shoes, and give away the excess.
6. Wash nylons and place in divided compartments for easy retrieval.
7. Sort and simplify everyone's sock drawers (one person a week).
8. Fold and restock everyone's underwear (one person a week).
9. Clean out and dust your nightstand and dresser tops.
10. Simplify the medicine cabinet.

You get the idea—keep organizing the "little things" to make a big difference. You'll feel so happy the next time you open an organized drawer that you'll say, "I own this space!" The secret is to do this at a regular time each week so that you won't forget.

	P Project	u (You)	S System	H Habit
Katie	• Get laundry under control.	• Master the same-day laundry principle.	• Simplify laundry needs. • Have a consistent schedule.	• Do the wash on regular days. • Keep tops of the washer and dryer clear.
Myrna	• Organize closets and simplify.	• Practice the fabulous 52-week system to keep closets and drawers simple.	• Hang all clothes in their proper category. • Utilize a give-away bag or basket in your closet.	• Wear what you like and love. • Put clothes away instead of putting them down.

Final Thought

A laundry system should be simple, straightforward, and leave your home looking clutter-free. The laundry baskets get put away, and the tops of the washer and dryer become as polished as the dining room table. The system is truly simple once you take the time to plan it out and use it.

The time you save getting ready each morning is worth the extra effort to get everything put away in one day. Clutter-free, organized closets invite you and your family to look your best. And simply put, an organized laundry system and closets relieve stress because everything is in its place before you start your day.

Personal Reflection

Ask yourself the following questions to see where you rate:

_____ 1. Is your laundry folded and put away?

_____ 2. Are the tops of your washer and dryer clear right now?

_____ 3. Do you know how many loads of wash you do each week?

_____ 4. Are your clothes clean and ready to wear whenever you need them?

_____ 5. Do you regularly give clothes away to a charity for people who need them?

If you answered yes to all the above questions, your systems are all working, and you have a simplified life in this area.

A final thought: Does it matter if your laundry is folded and put away the same day it's washed? You bet it does. Just check the stress level of your family the next morning when you don't.

> Completed laundry + an organized closet =
> Time saved and a wonderful sense of accomplishment!

A Simple Prayer of Love in Action

Dear God, You know there are baskets of laundry waiting to be folded and put away. When I face the laundry and closet disarray, remind me that helping my family dress their best is a way I can show them I love them. Help me to care for others with my actions and not just my words. Amen.

. . . .

Of course, we would all like to be appreciated and effective at the same time. If you have to choose between the two, be effective and let God be the One who appreciates you.

—PAM FARREL, _A Woman God Can Use_

eight

. . . .

The Third System:
Conquer Cleaning and Clutter

Make it a habit to give the house a quick pickup every day. Getting rid of the clutter will make you think it is cleaner than it really is.

—STEPHANIE CULP
You Can Find More Time for Yourself Every Day

ith great determination, Carolyn decided *this* would be the day to clean the whole house. Since the kids were at school, she was sure she could get everything done before three o'clock.

Even though the breakfast dishes were still on the kitchen table, she wanted to get going. She started vacuuming in the farthest corner of the family room until she hit a stack of newspapers next to the couch. *Better get these out of here now*, she mused.

As she opened the recycling lid in the garage, she spied a jumble of winter boots lying on the floor. She straightened them out and was delighted to find her missing glove. With triumph, she made a beeline to the front closet to put the lost glove back where it rightfully belonged.

Carolyn then noticed a laundry basket full of dirty clothes sitting at the top of the stairs. She carried the basket to the laundry room and tossed the load in. But as she pulled on the light switch string over the washing machine, the bulb burned out. *Not a problem. I'm getting a lot done today, and I can fix that, too*, she thought.

93

As she headed to the basement door to find a new light bulb, Carolyn noticed the breakfast dishes still on the table and the vacuum sitting in the family room. "Now who made this mess and left the vacuum in the middle of the floor?" she muttered as she marched down the stairs.

Impacts of Cleaning

Watching Carolyn clean house may make us chuckle, but we all can identify with someone who starts cleaning yet ends up with a bigger mess on her hands. Being pulled off track results in a less-than-satisfying outcome to anyone intent on sprucing up the well-loved place we call home.

When Carolyn called me, we started to discuss where cleaning fits into a woman's life. We agreed that her family would probably prioritize meals first, laundry second, and cleaning third. But for most women, a clean home is a higher priority because of the sense of peace and order it brings.

Carolyn was stuck on not only how to get the cleaning done without creating more of a mess, but also with the "Why do it?" aspect behind every pile she encountered. "Sometimes I think I clean for the family," she began, "but other times I dive in because I can't stand it anymore. That's where I get stuck. If nobody in the family says anything, are my cleaning efforts really worth it?"

My Story

I empathized with Carolyn and said I could really relate. "When we were first married, I recalled that 'cleaning for company' as a child meant dusting everything," I said. "So as a new bride, I dusted the house to impress my husband. Then David came home from work and asked me, 'What did you do all day?' Obviously, my dusting went over like a lead balloon.

"A week later, I quickly finished vacuuming as my husband pulled up. When he opened the door and looked around, he said, 'Wow, you cleaned the whole house!' A light bulb went on for me—and I gave up dusting for vacuuming. I determined to clean things that would make an impact, not just what should be done."

"I see," Carolyn said.

"Good. So if it's okay with you, Carolyn, let's look at creating a system that will make the most impact in the least amount of time," I continued. "Let's begin with two assumptions: First, we want a clean house that will meet our family, personal, and company needs. And second, we want cleaning systems that will work in the least amount of time."

Carolyn agreed that's what she wanted, so we began by looking at three aspects of cleaning:

1. Daily pick-up system
2. Weekly maintenance schedule
3. "Clean up clutter" projects as needed

These systems would help us achieve the best results with the least amount of time and effort.

· ·

There are two things going on. People are doing less housework because they don't have the time. But they're very concerned about how their homes look.

—MARY ELLEN PINKHAM, household hints expert

· ·

Daily Pick-Up—Saves Time or Takes Time?

The daily pick-up is an invaluable system for staying on top of our everyday mess-making activities. The daily pick-up should become a habit, just like brushing your teeth. There are two parts to this: morning and evening.

Morning Pick-Up

Each morning, start in your bedroom by making the bed and putting away pajamas and other clothes. Have each family member do the same in their bedrooms, though they will need help if they are six years of age or under. Next, move to the bathroom to briefly straighten towels, put away toothbrushes and makeup, and wipe off the counters and mirrors.

After picking up the bedrooms and bathrooms following breakfast, move on to the kitchen. Clear off the kitchen table, leaving only your attractive centerpiece. Put away all food, immediately clean up the dishes and wipe down the counters. You are now finished with the morning portion of the daily pick-up.

MORNING PICK-UP

Goal: *Everyone dressed, bedrooms picked up, and bathrooms and kitchen area cleaned.*

1. Make sure all beds are made.   2. Pick up the bathrooms.   3. Clean up the kitchen.

Evening Pick-Up

In the evening, the main pick-up goals should be to read the mail, put away the last load of laundry, and finish cleaning up in the kitchen. Also before dinner, make sure that everyone clears their belongings and papers from the family room, kitchen table, and entryway.

If these areas are cleared before dinner, you can spend the rest of the evening as you wish. If you are at work or gone during the day, try to finish these tasks early in the evening so you will still have time for yourself.

EVENING PICK-UP

Goal: *Bring closure to the day's tasks.*

1. Complete the day's mail.   2. Put away all laundry.   3. Pick up clutter spots.

My Home Looks Nice and I Feel Good

One of my class participants wrote back about the benefits of doing the daily pick-up: "Marcia, the daily pick-up system that I now do each morning has dramatically changed the appearance of my home! People actually think I've been cleaning for hours. The truth is, I've just done a few things. It's amazing what your system does to make my home look nice and to help me feel good."

Daily pick-up is not a big deal if you know it's part of your morning and evening routine. In the morning the three main traffic areas are the bedrooms, bathrooms, and kitchen. In the evening, the three similar traffic areas are the kitchen, family room, and mail/paper trail areas.

Expect to do the daily pick-up morning and evening, and accept it as a small time investment for a peaceful, orderly home. It takes less time than you think.

A Daily and Weekly Cleaning System

	MONDAY	TUESDAY	WEDNESDAY	THURSDAY	FRIDAY	SATURDAY	SUNDAY
A.M.	———————————————— Work ————————————————					Cleaning and Errands	Worship
P.M.	———————————————— Work ———————————————— ———————— Family/Dinner/Cleanup ————————					Laundry (4 loads)	
eve		GROCERY	Laundry (3 loads)	GROCERY		GROCERY	Plan for Week

Personal Time Management (A & B weekly schedule)

	MONDAY	TUESDAY	WEDNESDAY	THURSDAY	FRIDAY	SATURDAY	SUNDAY
WEEK A	1. Wash shirts 2. Iron	1. Change towels 2. Groceries	Kitchen floor	1. Vacuum 2. Green bath	Change towels	Projects as needed	Worship
ALWAYS	* Beds made (and bedrooms clean) in morning before breakfast. * Laundry put away before meals. * 6 P.M. dinner. Consistently clean up kitchen immediately after each meal.						
WEEK B	1. Wash whites 2. Change beds	1. Wash all towels 2. Groceries	Kitchen floor	1. Vacuum 2. Blue bath	Change towels	Projects as needed	Worship

Weekly Cleaning Keeps You Afloat

Carolyn was willing to try the daily pick-up, but she also wanted to move on to the rest of the house. "Yes, I admit that I get sidetracked going through the normal day's tasks. How exactly do I handle the rest of the house?" she asked.

"Carolyn, there are tasks that can keep your household afloat with minimal effort. These tasks, when done on a regular basis, will keep quick cleaning jobs from turning into major projects. Let's write out a weekly cleaning schedule that will work and move you in the right direction with minimal effort. The beauty of this approach is that you can simply write it on a three-by-five card and adjust it whenever your schedule changes."

Weekly Cleaning System

The weekly cleaning system is the backbone of staying on top of cleaning. Weekly cleaning frees up time because you create the time slot and systems that meet your needs. The goal is to stay ahead of the dust and clutter before it becomes obvious to you and everyone who lives there.

Here's what you do in the weekly cleaning:

1. Empty wastebaskets. Believe it or not, this is a sign of all clean homes and offices. Get your money's worth from your weekly garbage pick-up by tossing out everything you can.
2. Change bed linens. Instead of tackling the herculean task of changing all the beds on the same day, try changing no more than two beds per day. Set up a schedule for changing bed linens on a weekly or every-other-week schedule.
3. Vacuum. Vacuuming is one of the quickest ways to give the illusion of a clean home. It also minimizes dust and adds longevity to an expensive part of your home—your carpet and floors.
4. Clean kitchen and bathroom floors. When kitchen and bathroom floors are clean, people will presume you have a clean home. And all you did was keep the crumbs and dirt picked up.
5. Eliminate an annoying pile. Piles are telltale signs of disorder. How many do you see around your house right now? Conquer one pile per week, and soon you'll regain control.
6. Create a "Ten-Item Priority Project List." Jot down this priority project list while vacuuming and scrutinizing your home. List no more than ten items, though. Complete one project from your list each week before you add another.
7. Handle errands. Whenever possible, do a few errands on your way home from being out. A convenient, quick stop on the way home takes less time than getting up the momentum to go out and tackle a group of errands later.

THE WEEKLY CLEANING SYSTEM

Goal: *Stay ahead of cleaning and clutter with key tasks each week.*

1. Empty wastebaskets
2. Change bed linens.

3. Vacuum traffic areas.

4. Clean the kitchen and bathroom floors.

5. Eliminate an annoying pile.

6. Complete a project from the ten-item priority project list.

7. Include errand time for banking, gas, and shopping in your weekly plan.

Carolyn liked the idea of doing strategic weekly cleaning. Now there was hope to manage the essentials of the day and week. Together, we made out a weekly schedule, and she posted one inside her bathroom mirror and another in her kitchen at the personal organizing center. All it took was a quick look to remind her what she needed to do to stay on track and not let major cleaning overwhelm her again.

Clean-Up-Clutter Projects

Carolyn still had questions for me, however. "But how will I ever get beyond my daily routine to my cleaning and clutter projects? Is there a difference?" she asked.

"There is a difference between regular cleaning and cleaning up clutter," I replied. "Cleaning is the dusting, vacuuming, and floor mopping that you do on a daily or weekly schedule to keep your house clean."

Cleaning up clutter is dealing with all the items we dust and vacuum around—piles of videos, CDs, and cassettes in the family room; cardboard boxes; and notebooks of committee meetings and photo projects stacked up in corners. All these need to be dealt with to have a clean home and a simpler lifestyle.

These project piles will continue to grow and grow until you deal with them. You need to either find a "home" to put them away, do them, or return them to the store with their receipt. A simple lifestyle does not have piles!

Clean-up-clutter projects relate to anything not being handled in the cleaning schedule. Once these projects are dealt with, the daily pick-up becomes much easier. It's worth the effort to do one weekly clean-up-clutter project on the appropriate day of your cleaning routine.

The next time Carolyn vacuumed, she made a similar list of ten things that had become her personal clean-up-clutter projects. She had always made lists, but things never got done. Now she was thinking about her motivations to follow through on a project. The alternative was to fuss and fume about all the clutter at home. She decided to get going on her list and clean up her home—for good.

Clean-Up-Clutter Project Day	Time	My Motivations to Take Action
1. Wash the light fixtures.	10 minutes each	I love when they sparkle!
2. Scale down the number of refrigerator magnets.	10 minutes	This action makes the kitchen look cleaner and bigger.
3. Sort and purge the videos.	1 hour	Videos take up a lot of space and often get watched just once.
4. Organize all the books in the house.	2 hours	Someone else can be using them.
5. Clean off the fireplace mantel.	30 minutes	Dusty knickknacks depress me.
6. Organize the hall closet.	3 hours	I can't find anything anymore.
7. Clean up the bedroom piles.	30 minutes per pile	I really want to wake up to a clean room each morning.
8. Clean up the nightstand.	45 minutes	It would be so peaceful to have flowers with a book to read.
9. Sort the magazines.	30 minutes	I'd like to sit and read a magazine for relaxation.
10. Catch up on the to-read pile.	1 hour	Newspapers and magazine piles make any house look messy.

A True Sense of Order—Shelves and Drawers

Another way to de-clutter your home is to organize your shelves and drawers. Doing so will bring a true sense of order to your home. It is helpful to start here because each shelf and drawer is a defined space. Once you have conquered these small spaces, you will feel confident enough to move on to larger spaces.

Clean Shelves First

To begin organizing a shelf, take out all of the items and set them neatly aside. Then wipe off the shelf and add new shelf paper, if necessary. Choose attractive paper that can be maintained easily.

Throw away outdated and useless things, such as old food and outdated cosmetics, and you'll experience instant gratification. Sometimes you have to let go of old, familiar "stuff" to simplify your life.

Before returning an item to the shelf, decide whether you really need it. Think about whether the item should be

- kept,
- tossed,
- given away.

Then put back only what you like or are confident that you'll use. Put away all items with the labels facing forward. It helps to arrange items from tallest to shortest. Same-sized items are best arranged alphabetically. Leave one-third of the shelf space clear for simplicity and growth.

In general, you will feel more organized if you have clean shelves because you use them every day.

Personal Satisfaction—an Organized Drawer

To organize drawers follow the above steps for shelves. Put smaller items in open containers to keep them from sliding around. Shoeboxes or cardboard boxes cut to drawer height work great. And remember to put the most frequently used items in the front third of the drawer.

Kitchen towels and washcloths should be individually rolled or folded in shallow drawers so that each one can be seen and easily removed. Do the same with your silky clothing, but you might want to put them in a smaller container within the drawer.

Important: Only organize one drawer or shelf at a time and always start with a clean surface nearby. Then proceed to the next drawer. You are finished when you have put away or given away the piles you created.

In no time you will experience the gratification of opening an organized drawer. This will encourage you to move on to the other drawers and shelves in your house and even your garage! Work with that momentum and keep going.

Finding Time to Organize

Now that you know the "how to" of organizing, where do you find the time to organize shelves and drawers? The answer: either as you use them, or at a separate time. If you decide to do one refrigerator shelf a night, start at the top and work down. When you scrub down a bathroom, first organize a shelf or drawer and then continue with your bathroom cleaning. If you work better staying focused on one project, go for it and clean out all your bedroom drawers in one weekend.

The key is getting started and keeping your momentum going. When you're done with a certain area, reward yourself by buying a new organizing item for that area. This will help keep you motivated as you see the transformation of each shelf and drawer.

Task Oriented versus Goal Oriented

Making a list of clean-up-clutter projects gets you only halfway there. Why is that? Because it's just a list. And even if you go the next step and add a date and time frame to do it, you still might not get it done in a timely manner, if at all. Why does that happen? The answer lies in vision and action.

There are two perspectives:

- Task oriented: A woman who is task oriented has a long list of cleaning projects, but they may not be getting done because there is always more to do.

- Goal oriented: A goal-oriented woman has a vision of a clean, clutter-free home with time off to enjoy it. She does the right thing at the right time and for no longer than she intends to.

When You Don't Feel Like Cleaning

I once saw a saying in a gift shop that sums up how many women feel about cleaning: "I clean every other day. This is not the other day!"

Although we might have the same attitude, we still have to clean—whether we're in a bad mood or a good mood or in no mood. Wear comfortable clothing and tennis shoes, which can put a spring in your step as you wheel that vacuum around the house. Never try to clean in your pajamas or bathrobe, or you will take twice as long and never really finish.

When you are weary and need to clean, perk yourself up by putting on your favorite high-energy music. At the very least, you'll burn some calories if you work energetically until the windows sparkle and the clutter is put away.

If all else fails, talk to yourself. Tell yourself what a great job you're doing and what fun it will be to sit down and read a magazine when you finally put the dust rag away for the week.

Ten Tips to Simplify Your Cleaning

1. Start cleaning after the daily pick-up is finished.
2. Clean the visible and obvious messes first.
3. Do tasks that will give you visible results and personal satisfaction.
4. Get rid of the dirt on the largest surfaces—floors and counters.
5. Use a timer and find out how little time a task takes.
6. Do routine tasks the same day of the week, and don't worry about them until then.
7. Recognize cleaning has a beginning and an end; focus on the end result.
8. Beautify what you do so clean is more appealing than cluttered.
9. Make a clean sweep through the house each night so you begin each day with a fresh start.
10. Take Sunday off so you have a day to look forward to—a day of rest.

Benefits of Being Organized

Once you know how to clean up effectively, it's important to remind yourself of the benefits awaiting you. A simple cleaning system gives you

- a nice-looking home,
- more free time,
- less stress.

Anything that becomes routine takes less physical and emotional energy. Always remember an organized home is easier to maintain than a disorganized home. It is definitely worth the time to create a system that works for you.

As you continue to make a clean sweep throughout your home, you will get better and better at it. It will take less time. And the payoff comes when you find out how easy it becomes to stay on top of the dust and clutter.

Is Cleaning Worth My Time?

Carolyn, I'm happy to say, got the picture. "This 'dive right in' approach is for the birds. I have too much to do in life to waste any time. I am on the road to a new life and a clean house," she concluded emphatically. "I know my family will benefit, but I really want a weekly plan just for my own peace of mind." She knew she was getting organized about cleaning for herself, not just for company or the family.

As Carolyn wondered whether she could get everything done that we talked about, I reminded her of an important principle from the Bible: "The wise woman builds her house, but . . . the foolish one tears hers down" (Proverbs 14:1). This means the wise woman persistently invests in improving her home, while the foolish or impulsive woman tears hers apart.

We shared a good laugh that the principle was so appropriate as we viewed the disarray of the family room, laundry, and garage all in process at once.

Carolyn chuckled again at her morning efforts as she grabbed her calendar and wrote out a room-per-day plan over the next week. She was ready to get going with her new focus, and it wasn't even lunchtime yet. Now where was that vacuum?

Personal Reflection

1. What do you most enjoy about a clean home?

   _____

2. What is the most frustrating part of cleaning your home?

   _____

3. What cleaning habit would make the biggest and most dramatic improvement in your home?

   _____

4. What three words do you want to reflect the clean feeling of your home?

_____ _____ _____

A Simple Prayer of Perseverance

Dear God, thank You for a roof over my head and a place to call home. Help me to keep at the cleaning and clutter pick-ups so my home becomes my castle. Help me to persevere and stay focused. I am grateful that at least You and I know what I did today. Amen.

. . . .

A good 50 percent of housework is not just cleany-clean, scrubby-scrubbing, but shuffling clutter, litter, and junk from place to place. Getting rid of junk is the easiest way to free yourself from household imprisonment.

—DON ASLETT, *Clutter's Last Stand*

nine

The Fourth System:
Power Through Projects

Remember, stress does not come from being busy. Stress comes from being busy about things we don't want to do, or from not being busy about things we do want to do.

—PATRICIA SPRINKLE
Women Who Do Too Much

Every once in a while I run into a competent woman who just gets "stuck." Pam fit into that category: capable and accomplished, but bogged down. One afternoon we got together for coffee at Starbucks, where she started to pour out her heart.

"I'm thinking about a lot of things I would like to do," she began, "but I just can't seem to get going on any of them. My photos need to be put into albums, I've always wanted to redecorate my bedroom, and our yard is in pretty sad shape. I can't get myself started on anything. My bigger dream has always been to go to Hawaii, but that is looking out of sight, too. It's not that I don't have time to do these things because I do. And I'm not even sure it's money holding me back. Actually, it's something inside me that just can't take that step to get going."

"You look pretty frustrated," I empathized.

"Yes, I am," she said with some emphasis. "One of my friends just redid her kitchen, my other friend went to visit her daughter in Florida for two weeks, and another friend just got new carpeting. Why can't I get myself to do any of these things?" she said with tears welling up in her eyes. "What do they have that I don't?"

Changing the Status Quo

Pam's question was a very good one, and what she was really asking was this: How do I become a person who makes things happen, especially if I have to be the one to do it?

For each person the answer is different, but basically all the answers boil down to this: You must want change more than you want the status quo. When that happens, we can create the know-how, the steps, and the momentum to get it done. That's when anything is possible. Oftentimes a woman needs to be reminded that she is not as helpless as she feels.

I could tell this was really weighing on Pam, so we began talking about it. Pam was thinking everyone else had it together but her. That simply was not true. Everyone has something they want to get around to. Her friends were just ready and prepared to make that happen. And we were going to get Pam ready, too.

After more discussion, we made a list of her dreams on the back of a restaurant napkin. Pam left Starbucks that afternoon with her spirits renewed. She had made many wonderful changes before. She could do it again. She just needed to get back on track. Here are some of the ideas I shared with her.

Powering Through Projects

"Powering through" projects is the secret to creating the momentum to bring about positive change. It is the vision and energy carrying us from the beginning of an idea to the completion of a desire. Projects take deliberate effort and are the lifeblood of changing your life.

POWERING THROUGH PROJECTS

Projects are tasks outside your daily routine that make life easier, accomplish something of value, or prepare you for your future.

"Powering through" is the momentum to start and finish a project. It is about finding the desire to move ahead and removing the obstacles that hold you back.

Most problems in doing a project are twofold:

- Taking risks to pursue a project
- Knowing how to engage and complete a project

If you acquire the skill of powering through projects, you can simplify your lifestyle sooner than you think. Then you can initiate change anytime you want.

Your Project Quotient (Your P. Q.)

If you are feeling like Pam, you may need to look at your recent history of taking on new projects. In the questions below, write in A, B, C, D, or E to reflect the last time you did the project in question:

Answer Key

A. 1–3 months ago   C. 1–3 years ago   E. never
B. 4–12 months ago   D. 3–10 years ago

When was the last time you

_____ 1. bought a new outfit and wore it?

_____ 2. returned an item and got your money back?

_____ 3. invited company over for dinner?

_____ 4. took a vacation?

_____ 5. got a new hairstyle?

_____ 6. redecorated a room at your house?

_____ 7. washed and vacuumed your car?

_____ 8. completed your taxes before March 30?

_____ 9. put money in a savings account?

_____ 10. wrote down a list of dreams for the rest of your life?

Where Do You Rate?

If the majority of your answers were in the A and B categories, you have a good chance of accomplishing more projects very soon.

If most of your answers were in the C, D, and E range, you need to get your momentum going again.

Your answers are an indicator of three things:

- How rusty you are at making changes in your life
- How well you follow through on things you initiate
- How much thought you have put into your next couple years

If it has been a while since you have made a change, you need some practice to work up to bigger changes. Here's the plan. I will teach you how to do small, medium, and large projects. When we are finished, I have no doubt that you will be able to accomplish any project you set out to do.

Projects: Your Choice

At any given time, we have to fit specific projects into our lives. Just for fun, check off what size project you would consider each of these:

	Small	Medium	Large
Painting a room	_____	_____	_____
Weeding the garden	_____	_____	_____
Cleaning the garage	_____	_____	_____
Shampooing the carpets	_____	_____	_____
Hosting a birthday party	_____	_____	_____
Framing pictures	_____	_____	_____
Organizing photos	_____	_____	_____
Doing your taxes	_____	_____	_____
Having a garage sale	_____	_____	_____
Shopping for Christmas presents	_____	_____	_____
Cleaning out e-mails	_____	_____	_____
Getting a broken clock repaired	_____	_____	_____
Refinishing furniture	_____	_____	_____
Purchasing a new appliance	_____	_____	_____
Dealing with finances	_____	_____	_____

_____	___	___	___
_____	___	___	___
_____	___	___	___
_____	___	___	___

Add some of your own projects on the blank lines. Then put a star by all the projects you would personally like to do.

Worthwhile Projects

Once you identify what projects intrigue you, the next step is to determine whether the project is worth doing. Ask yourself:

- What steps would I have to take to afford the time and money involved to do it?
- Would this be a major or minor interruption to my life?
- Would the benefits outweigh the obstacles?

But my favorite question is this:

- If I don't do this project, how long am I willing to live with this as it is?

When I asked my real-estate agent if we should remodel the master bathroom, she wisely said, "If you are going to be here longer than two years, then yes. That way it will benefit the resale, and you will get to enjoy it as well." That is usually the motivation to do something sooner rather than later—it benefits you now and later.

Small, Medium, and Large Projects

Recognize the time frame of the project and see where it will fit in your life.
- Small: 15 minutes–a full day
  Example: cleaning out a shelf, a set of drawers, or a pantry
- Medium: 4 days–4 weeks
  Example: organizing a whole closet, bedroom, or kitchen
- Large: 1–6 months
  Example: redecorating a bedroom, organizing the garage, or redoing your filing system

Small Projects: Success in a Nutshell

Doing small projects can build the momentum for tackling larger ones. Warm up your project skills by completing something small that will simplify your life.

For example:

- Simplify your purse by tossing receipts and corralling useful "little stuff" into a Ziploc bag.

- Clean out the kitchen junk drawer and keep quality items, not junk, in there.

- Spend five minutes and polish your favorite shoes.

- Clean out your makeup drawer by washing the hairbrushes and getting rid of old lipsticks and nail polishes.

- Use up laundry samples.

- Simplify your pantry by donating food items no one eats.

- Give the garbage cans a good scrub so they look clean.

I know of several success stories:

- One lady, who got frustrated losing her keys when it was time to leave, bought a key hook that day and hung it herself.

- A minister got tired of writing out his sermons with any old pen. Instead of putting up with it any longer, he stopped in the middle of writing a sermon and went out and purchased a good quality pen that he was pleased with.

- A busy mom got her photos organized by buying drawers for her pictures and tossing the boxes that always had clutter sitting on the tops.

- An office manager confessed she spent the weekend sorting and purchasing the right color nylons just to make the workweek go smoother.

These people know the value of tackling small projects to simplify their personal stressors. It's a great feeling opening your kitchen drawer to find a working pen and a pad of paper to take down a phone message.

Small Projects: Time and Benefits

Don't overlook the long-term value of doing smaller projects. These projects will reduce stress and simplify your life today. This is the time to go back to the clean-up clutter projects in the last chapter and follow through. Those small projects will make your life a breeze.

Your time frame to do a project should be no longer than two hours or fifteen minutes daily over a week or two. It's amazing how good you'll feel from organizing one small area that you use quite often.

Medium Projects: The Black Hole

When you ignore small projects around you, they can turn into medium-sized projects seemingly overnight and become a big headache. Plenty of folks have tons of stuff in cardboard boxes that they vow to deal with later, but later never comes—until they finally decide to do something, like Jennifer did.

Jennifer lived in a mobile home and put everything she didn't know what to do with on her screened-in porch. When Jennifer called me to organize this extended storage area, my first question was, "What do you call this room?"

"I don't tell anyone, but secretly my daughter and I call it 'the black hole,'" she whispered with a laugh.

"Well, first we have to change its name," I insisted. After some debate, Jennifer's eyes lit up. "I know—let's call it the 'sun porch,'" she said.

We rolled up our sleeves and spent the first weekend going through boxes, most of which contained old items that could be tossed or given away. Her new vision of how she would use the room carried her through sorting all the old boxes, bags, and clutter. The next weekend, Jennifer purchased attractive but inexpensive furniture. During the summer months, she and her daughter began eating dinner outside. After years of accumulation and dread, it only took two weekends to transform a cluttered catchall into an attractive porch by Memorial Day.

Large Projects: Deciding Which One First

You could probably sit down right now and write out a list of at least a dozen large projects that you'd like to get done around the house. These projects require thought and persistence, so it's important to plan carefully.

My friend Mary is a perfect example. She was fed up with the clutter in her garage and the decorating in her bedroom. She was also discouraged by the time and energy it would take to get both areas to look and feel the way she wanted. Mary, like many of us, had limited time to devote to home projects. She worked during the day and had family commitments that filled her nights and weekends.

We discussed the importance of choosing one priority at a time, which meant either the garage or the bedroom had to be first. She also needed to check her schedule and determine how realistic it was to fit both in. Did she have a special event coming up during which she would want to show off her new bedroom? Or was it more important to fit all of the cars in the garage before winter?

That which we persist in doing becomes easier—not that the nature of the task has changed, but our ability to do it has increased.

—RALPH WALDO EMERSON

Large Project: Redecorating the Master Bedroom

Mary decided to take on the master bedroom project first and have it done by her anniversary in four weeks. She decided to do it herself rather than hiring it out, even though she worked full-time. The first week she got her creative juices flowing by scouting out some model homes, a decorating center, the mall, and paint stores.

In the second week, Mary spent lunch hours and after work "just checking out a few more things." The power of an enthusiastic woman was unrelenting. Soon her friends were involved in her anniversary project and helped her locate a bedspread and drapes—on sale, of course!

Mary's third weekend was devoted to manual labor. She began painting, and her husband and friends pitched in, so it felt like a party.

The fourth and final week was the most fun, as she put it all together and purchased final accessories. She picked out new towels and a bath mat on Monday. Then she found new soap dispensers, drinking glasses, and pictures that completed the accessories. By Thursday night, everything was ready in time for the anniversary weekend. She enjoyed a double bonus—she finished the master bedroom in time for the anniversary and could enjoy it for years to come.

In just one month, Mary decorated her bedroom and created a beautiful retreat. She also created energy and enthusiasm that spilled over into other parts of her life and got her friends motivated as well.

Large Project: Organizing the Garage

Mary's excitement began to wane when she thought about cleaning the garage, however. When she began to visualize getting the garage back under control, her spirits lifted. Mary tackled one wall per weekend, and before she knew it, the garage was finally done. Each time she drove into the garage, Mary felt new energy and enthusiasm. She was glad to know that the garage items she gave away were benefiting others and now the remaining things were easier to find.

Organizing your garage, attic, basement, or spare room begins with several simple steps. Beginning at the entrance to the area, start creating a path through the center, attending to each item as you encounter it.

Your choices are

- Toss broken or old items. Make sure you have a large wastebasket or recycling container at your side.

- Give away useful items. Put them into boxes or bags marked for the organization or person who will receive the items. Then, make sure you actually donate your used items right away, or they will pile up somewhere else in your house.

- Put away items that you plan to keep. You might want to build or buy special organizing systems for the walls or closets. Then put things away so that they are easy to find and get to.

If you make sure to do it right the first time, you won't be going back every few months to do it all over again.

Next, after the center of the room is reclaimed, go back to the entrance and systematically go around the perimeter of the room, making a decision to toss, give away, or put away each item.

TALK OUT LOUD AS YOU ORGANIZE

The toughest part of organizing a garage, attic, basement, or spare room is to stay on task. Professional organizers can do it for or with you and speed up the process because

---

they are trained in space management. They work with people to see "old" things in a new way. But if you would rather do it yourself, here are some important questions to ask regarding each item.

1. Do I use it?
2. Do I like it?
3. Would I be happier if someone else were storing it or putting it to good use?
4. If I were moving, would I pay to have it packed and moved?
5. Would my life be happier without this?
   (If improved, then you know what to do—let it go!)

Motivating Yourself

One way you can motivate yourself is to snap a "before" picture and compare it to a magazine layout of a well-decorated master bedroom or a clean garage. Then work to make that vision a reality. Often just the picture of a new color scheme, window treatment, or bedspread will motivate you to tackle a project.

Another tip is to tell lots of people that you are going to do a project. That motivates you to stand behind your statement. The social pressure could be just the catalyst you need. Your friends will be asking if you finished, so you will have to follow through to get it done. There are no prizes for just talking about projects, but there are big rewards for seeing things through to the end.

Rewards for Getting Your Projects Done

One of the challenges to get yourself going is finding your motivation. I once asked a class of mine why they would want to accomplish their projects. Here are some of their answers:

- "I wouldn't have to waste time looking for things."
- "Things will look much neater."
- "I'll have more time to play with the kids."
- "Our home will be nicer for the family."
- "I'll be a happier person."

Do projects make a difference? You bet they do, especially if you can reap one of the above rewards.

Multitasking Projects

Pam called back a week later, just as she had promised. She had decided to go for a small-, medium-, *and* large-sized project. Her big project would be redecorating her kitchen with new countertops, paint, and wallpaper. She had visited at least six kitchen showrooms and had already ordered the kitchen countertop.

While she was waiting for her new countertop to be made and fitted, she worked on a small personal project—organizing her bedroom drawers and closet shelves. Each day she worked on a new drawer, and the pile of things to give away to charity grew. "I just love my room now," she said. "I had wanted to do this for a long time, so it feels good to go through everything and simplify the amount of stuff I wake up to every morning."

When she was finished with her bedroom, Pam tackled the granddaddy of all organizing projects, the garage. "I don't know what I'll find, but I am determined that this summer my garage will look decent. We'll get the cars in there, and I won't be embarrassed," she said.

"That's super. So what's your plan after that?" I asked.

"My plan after getting those two projects done is to get the photos together in the fall to display for the holidays," Pam replied. "My kids and husband will be really surprised and impressed. My motivation is that we're all planning to be together this year. It may not happen again for a long time, so I want it to be fun and memorable," she said.

"I'm unstuck! Now I'm going to start gathering information for my next year's goal— my trip to Hawaii! It's the big fiftieth birthday for my husband and me, and we're not getting any younger. I am going to do it!"

Personal Reflection

If you have found a project you can do easily, then do it. If there are obstacles to overcome but your passion is stronger, you still can do it. Enlist your friends or resource people who can help you get the job done.

One interior decorator said to me, "Marcia, I have never seen anyone get her husband to do as many projects as you do. How do you do it?"

I smiled and said, "Simple. I just limit my list to about three priority projects, and we talk together about how to do it. And then I thank him over and over after it's done. We both benefit that way."

1. Is there a project that you should finish up or even abort before moving forward?
   _____

2. If you had the choice of doing some meaningful small projects, what would they be?
   _____

3. If you could improve your life by doing several medium projects in a row, what would they be?
   _____

4. What big project would go a long way toward simplifying your life?
   _____

5. If you are very busy, what one project could you possibly do this year for a coming holiday?
   _____

> A project + motivation + time leverage = A clear path to success

A Simple Prayer to Follow Through

Dear God, one of the benefits of being a woman is our ability to plan ahead and dream of new things to do. Thanks for making us this way . . . and help me to follow through on the great ideas I come up with, or leave them aside for the right time in life. And don't forget, I wouldn't mind fastening my seat belt on a plane to Hawaii. Amen.

. . . .

The secret of getting ahead is getting started. The secret of getting started is breaking your complex overwhelming tasks into small manageable tasks, and then starting on the first one.

—MARK TWAIN, author

Simplify Special
Seasons of Life

Enjoy the special seasons of your life . . .

- Simplify Your Worklife

- Simplify Your Parenting

- Simplify the Holidays

- Simplify Your Transitions

ten

Simplify Your Worklife

Too often the desk becomes a place where things are waiting to happen;
instead, make it a place for action. . . . If you were a pilot, you wouldn't find
spare parts in the middle of the runway. They would be in the hangar. Get
out of the habit of keeping everything at your fingertips.

—SUSAN SILVER
Organized to Be the Best!

*I*t was Monday morning at 9 A.M., and Teresa quickly gathered her presentation folder as her first client rang the doorbell. Teresa, who was starting to work from home, was eager to do a good job. She had piles of new marketing materials, two boxes full of manila folders, and a brand-new computer. She gave her first presentation that morning, but that afternoon she called me and said, "I've never worked in an office environment before. Is there some special way I should be setting up my home-based business so I can actually make some income?" We set up an appointment and agreed to accomplish just that.

The next day her neighbor Regina called me during her lunch hour from city hall downtown. "I'm a city clerk," she began, "sitting in a typical cubicle with lots of people pulling at me and multiple projects going on. My boss is hinting that I need to get organized and said I should call you. What I want to know is, who cares if I cover my shelves with cartoons, tape my children's artwork to the walls, and write my projects on a scratch pad? I get the work done, right?"

I listened and agreed to work with Regina if she was open to learning some new tips. She said she was.

That same week I had an appointment with Joanne, an important businesswoman in the community, to organize her office. As I entered her less-than-tidy corner office with a view, she tucked her phone under her ear and frantically looked for a pen and a pad of paper to write on. Her frantic effort caused papers to swoosh over the desk and onto the floor. She hung up the phone and let out a sigh. "If I can't manage this better, I am going to have to look for another job. The stress is killing me."

The Three Lady Clients

All three women were in desperate need of organizing their workplace, and they needed help right away. The good news was that there were ways to streamline how they went about their work, but they just hadn't had the opportunity to learn them yet. They agreed that a lack of organization results in the stress of misplaced items, deadline pressures, and busyness without satisfaction.

Studies show that given the choice of offering a pay raise between two employees, managers tend to reward the more-organized employees. That in itself is a reason to get organized—and simplifying the stress at work is a close second.

How about You?

Before I describe what steps I had each client take to solve her problems, I want you to think about your desk and your productivity. I feel strongly that you can learn the same professional skills that a CEO uses to handle paperwork, whether you are paying the family bills, writing a business proposal, or filling out retirement forms. You deserve a well-designed desk to do your work, too.

Your desk can be the place where you earn your living or a place at home where you handle your filing and paper projects. Either way, there are six things you need to do to set up your desk properly:

Six Steps to Setting Up Your Work Area

1. *Simplify the top of your desk.* Stack papers into a neat pile or piles on one side of your desk. Work until you create a clear work space in the center of the desk. Get rid of any old Post-it notes and desk clutter. Take a moment to dust or wash the desktop, especially if it's been a while.

Mentally divide your desk in half horizontally. The half closest to you is the inner work space, while the back half is called the outer work space. Note that my desk diagram further divides these halves into six imaginary sections, which will help you strategically set up your work space. This system is effective for any work space including a countertop.

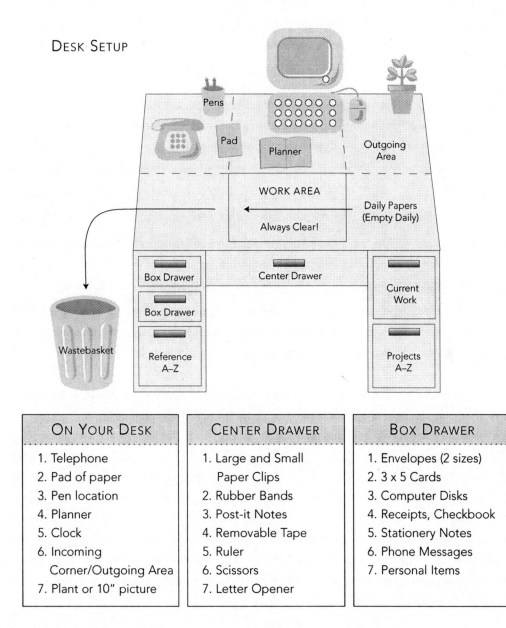

DESK SETUP

Pens

Pad

Planner

Outgoing Area

WORK AREA

Daily Papers (Empty Daily)

Always Clear!

Box Drawer

Center Drawer

Current Work

Box Drawer

Wastebasket

Reference A–Z

Projects A–Z

ON YOUR DESK	CENTER DRAWER	BOX DRAWER
1. Telephone	1. Large and Small Paper Clips	1. Envelopes (2 sizes)
2. Pad of paper	2. Rubber Bands	2. 3 x 5 Cards
3. Pen location	3. Post-it Notes	3. Computer Disks
4. Planner	4. Removable Tape	4. Receipts, Checkbook
5. Clock	5. Ruler	5. Stationery Notes
6. Incoming Corner/Outgoing Area	6. Scissors	6. Phone Messages
7. Plant or 10" picture	7. Letter Opener	7. Personal Items

Inner part of the desk: The three sections closest to you as you sit at your desk are called the inner part of the desk. They should contain your current work in the left-hand or right-hand corner as you sit down at your desk, a clear work space in the middle, and another clear space in the other front corner. It is important to keep the inner part of the desk organized and clean to focus on the work at hand.

Outer part of the desk: The back half of the desk is considered the outer part of the desk. This area generally includes your phone, your planner, a personal computer, and an outgoing corner.

To make the most of your desktop, designate one corner of your desk for incoming paperwork and projects. If you're wondering which corner to use, choose the corner that you pass when you sit down. Use a clearly marked "in-box," which will also help others know where to deposit items that need your attention. On the same side of the desk, designate the other corner for your "out-box," which you can use for outgoing paperwork like letters and reports.

- *Phone:* Position your phone so you pick it up with your nonwriting hand, then you can take notes as you talk. If you spend a lot of time on the phone, consider using a headset.

- *Personal planner:* Your personal planner or PDA needs to sit in one place, preferably at the top of your cleared work space. It should be left open to the current day and easily available so you can write down new tasks that come up.

- *Computer:* While it's important to place your computer in front of you, make every effort to maintain a sizable work space in front of you. Slide the keyboard under the monitor or under the desk on a keyboard tray when it's not in use.

2. *Streamline your desk drawers.* If you never open the small desk drawers, it's time to clean them out and get them back into use. Completely empty and refill one drawer at a time with only items that you'll need for your job.

The center drawer (or most accessible side drawer) should hold a divided desk tray. In that tray, you should have large and small paper clips in separate compartments, large and small Post-it notes, selected pens and pencils, scissors, rubber bands, removable tape, letter opener, stamps, and return address labels. You need only one ruler, stapler, and staple remover. Get rid of all the other clutter. For instance, if you don't have a bulletin board, why save pushpins?

You will need only a couple of your favorite pens, a pencil or two for writing items on your calendar, and a red pen to check off what you accomplish. Keep them in your center drawer or in a pencil holder.

3. Plow through your in-box. It may be tough to empty your in-box (or incoming corner) daily, but it is vital to your long-term success. It should take less than twenty minutes each day to deal with all of the incoming paperwork that arrives in your in-box. If you wait until the end of the week, it will take you two hours or longer to go through the accumulated material. Daily maintenance is always easier and more effective.

WORKSTATION OR "L" SETUP

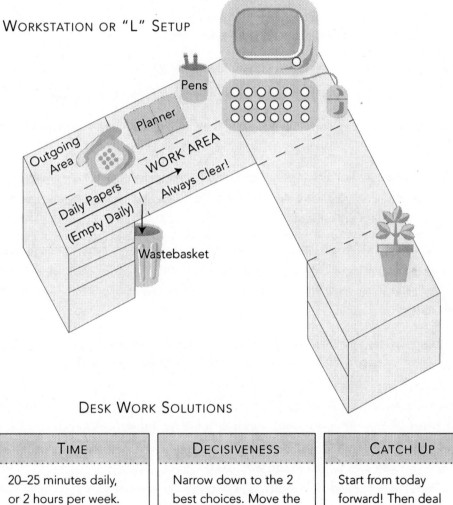

Pens

Planner

Outgoing Area

WORK AREA

Daily Papers

Always Clear!

(Empty Daily)

Wastebasket

DESK WORK SOLUTIONS

TIME	DECISIVENESS	CATCH UP
20–25 minutes daily, or 2 hours per week. Develop a regular daily habit.	Narrow down to the 2 best choices. Move the paper to the next step.	Start from today forward! Then deal with the backlog.

4. *Clean out your file drawers.* Before you run down to Office Depot and purchase another set of file drawers, weed out your existing files. Throw away old bills and paperwork. You may discover that you now have plenty of room for new files.

Rule of thumb: Leave four to six inches of extra space in every file drawer you clean out. Never try to squeeze "just one more" file into a drawer that is already full. You should be able to easily slide your hand in and out of a file drawer without scraping your knuckles. Your goal is to retreive any item within a minute.

Here are some tips for keeping your files under control:

- Always label a file in easy-to-read large, capital letters.

- Use only one to two words in a file name, and file it under the first word.

- Each file should hold no less than eight sheets of paper and no more than one inch of papers.

- Put new items in the front of the folder, and toss any no-longer-needed papers from the back of the file. If you consistently toss the same number you put in, you won't have to do a big file cleanout.

- When a hanging file gets too thick, divide the contents into three or four separate manila folders inside. Place them in alphabetical order (A–K, L–R, S–Z) or quarters of the year, such as January–March, April–June, July–September, and October–December.

Label each file drawer with one to two broad category topics such as Current Work, Clients, or A–Z Reference. Label every file drawer clearly and attractively.

5. *Deal with piles, bookshelves, and visible items.* Stand back from your work area and scan the desktop, bookshelves, and floor as if you are seeing everything for the first time. Does the area say to your visitors or clients that you have it together? You should be confident in your ability to get things done, and other people will have that same confidence in you if your work area is well organized.

Make sure your bookshelves, walls, and counters are clutter free and appealing to work around. Books and folders on your bookshelves should stand vertically. Never allow papers to pile up on the floor if you are planning to live a simplified lifestyle at work. Deliver, file, read, or toss piles until everything is off the floor.

FOUR STEPS TO DEAL WITH PAPER

Keep yourself focused by asking, "What is the next step for this piece of paper?" Here are my four options:

1. Read it and toss. Seventy to 80 percent of daily papers should be handled this way.
2. Deal with it now. Deal with new paper right away, if you can take care of it in five minutes or less. Or you can direct it to someone else with a Post-it note in the upper right-hand corner and put it in your out-box.
3. Master your to-do list. If a piece of paper requires attention in the near future, mark it in your personal planner and file it in your to-do folder. Then perform the task on the day you listed.
4. File it. Instead of piling more and more papers on your desk, file completed items under the appropriate heading (such as receipts or bills) or put papers that still need attention on your list and in your to-do file.

6. *Simplify your e-mail.* When you organize your office, consciously set up systems for your e-mail. The good news is it replaces time spent talking on the phone or in person. The bad news is our computer in-boxes have more inputs than our mailboxes and phone lines ever did!

To control your e-mail, count how much you get in a day and how many are left at the end of the day. For example, if you receive forty a day and delete only twenty, you will have 600 left in your in-box by the end of the month! That's too much stress and search time when you need an important item.

Establish time boundaries so e-mail doesn't consume your days. For example, don't open e-mail until you have spent a half-hour on paperwork. Then do like most people: open and respond in the morning, after lunch, and at the end of the day. If you continuously check your e-mail, you never get anything done. Estimate how much of your productive work time should be spent on e-mail and limit it to that.

Make Your Desk an Attractive Space

Although your desk needs to stay clear and organized, it should still reflect your personality. An attractive silk plant, a special clock, and a framed family photograph will provide the right personal and professional touch.

TIPS TO SIMPLIFY YOUR E-MAIL

- Do important action items immediately.
- Use the "delete" button for 70 percent of what comes in.
- Respond right away to personalized e-mails.
- Don't feel obligated to respond to forwards.
- Get off e-mail lists that no longer pertain to you.
- Stop responding when an interchange has served its purpose.
- Store dangling e-mails in folders like To Read, Holding, or a project name.
- Dealing with your e-mail is like dealing with paper: you need to control it, or it will control you.

The Two-Minute Desk Pick-Up

Manage your desk all day by practicing the "two-minute pick-up." That means, before you stand and walk away for a meeting or lunch, spend two minutes tying up loose ends, such as the following:

1. Clear off the center of your desk and jot down your next three action items for your return.
2. Straighten the papers you were working on and put away any files.
3. Enter new information into your database and toss scraps of paper.
4. Return pens, paper clips, and stapler to their rightful homes.
5. "Stairstep" your priority paperwork by putting the most important to-do items on top and the next ones showing under that.
6. Send an e-mail to move an action forward or respond to a question.
7. Prioritize telephone calls you need to make when you return.
8. Pencil-mark the spot where you stopped reading.
9. Clear away all clutter, and push in your chair.
10. Take items with you that can be delivered or mailed so that you can get them out of your work area.

Teresa and Her Home Office

Teresa, the client starting a home-based business, had the benefit of starting from scratch at a "new" office setup. She was experiencing clutter and confusion, however, because she didn't know which direction her business would go and what her setup needs would be.

Generally in a home-office setting, people need

- A desk with a computer and printer
- Small drawers to hold supplies
- Files and file drawers to hold paperwork
- Shelving for products and notebook binders
- A planner for action items
- A phone and answering machine
- A printer-fax-copier

I met with Teresa one afternoon and turned her paper piles into files and notebooks. "Don't worry about creating the perfect file system," I said, "since you can always change the names as you become familiar with the business. But do label the files knowing that the first word will be the one that it is filed under."

We set up hanging file names like Brochures, Business Information, Checking Account, Contacts, Distributors, Expenses, Forms, Leads, Preferred Customers, and Training.

Within each of these hanging files were three manila-tabbed folders that explained further divisions, such as

Leads: New	Leads: In Progress	Leads: Past

She hung her business chart and goals on the wall above her desk and a landscape picture on the room's largest wall. As I left, Teresa smiled as she looked around her office and dialed her next prospect.

Regina's Downtown Cubicle

Regina's desk at city hall was inside a cubicle, so she was already set up with equipment. In an effort to personalize her space, her work area overflowed with paperwork, children's artwork, and personal knickknacks. What remained was a cluttered hodgepodge.

"I think I could get more organized, but I am just really, really busy," she complained. "I also think the space is too small to make it look any better."

"Don't give up," I said. "There is always hope . . . and help."

We began by stacking all of her piles neatly on the side of her desk until we created a clear work space in the middle of the desk. After going through her pile of papers from the top down, we found her biggest need was a message system for incoming calls. Her best choices were either a notebook or the computer, but not scraps of paper!

After checking with a coworker who had a similar job, she learned that there was an excellent software program that she could use to manage incoming calls. With that problem solved, we turned our energies toward creating systems until the papers on the desk and floor were cleaned up.

For her children's artwork and personal knickknacks, I reminded Regina that a "less is more" approach is more professional. She attached two of her children's recent art projects to the side of her file cabinet that only she could see. She took home several older family photos and promised to replace them with a recently framed picture of her family.

In the very last pile, Regina was excited to find a missing file that her boss had been asking her about. She returned it with a bit of chagrin. "Okay, I get it," she confessed to me. "File it, but never pile it. I promise to be a new woman."

We slapped hands on a high-five as she settled back to work. The phone rang at her desk as I walked away. "Hello, this is Regina Williams," she said with a cheery voice. "You have reached city hall. How may I help you?"

Joanne's Office View

Joanne had a bigger office, more responsibility, and completely different needs. Yet we started in the same place—organizing her office, getting everything put away, and listing all her work that we uncovered.

"Now the good news is, I can see my desktop and I know where everything is," Joanne said proudly. "The bad news is, I found over twenty items to catch up on. How will I ever get them done?"

My concern for Joanne was not the long list of catch-up things to do; it was learning how to manage her day better. She needed to locate a planner and learn how to use it quickly. Fortunately, she had a planner on hand, and we began.

Since it was the end of the day, we wrote out her list of things to do for the following day and set them in place. Initially, she just wrote the ten-item to-do list below.

Ten-Item To-Do List for Work

- ❏ Meet with Big Al
- ❏ Pick up insurance forms from human resources (HR)
- ❏ Make appointment with Dr. Ross
- ❏ Client meeting with the Sullivans (9:00 A.M.)
- ❏ Seminar on time management (11:30–1:00)
- ❏ Finish file for Mr. Adams ASAP
- ❏ Urgent letter to Dave Johnson
- ❏ Order airline tickets for next month
- ❏ Pick up dry cleaning
- ❏ Reschedule Wednesday lunch

After making the list of key things to do, we scheduled them in her planner in this order:

1. Appointments
2. Priority Projects
3. Calls
4. Errands

Joanne was able to set up her day with time slots in her planner. "Wow, what a difference from a to-do list to mapping out your time for the day in a planner. Does this really work?" she asked.

"Yes, it does," I explained, "if you decide who is in control of your time—you or everything around you. When you decide you want to change your style from chaos to control, you can. Just keep practicing it every day—planning, doing, and evaluating—until you are in sync with your work."

Joanne was delighted with her clean office and her new time plan to get work done. She was actually visibly relieved. "You mean I can really schedule priorities in my day like that?" she asked, looking at her planner.

"Absolutely," I responded. "If you don't, you won't get on top of your work, and you will be constantly changing jobs looking for something better. 'Better' comes when you manage your current situation with ease."

TODAY'S DATE: APRIL 27		TIME EVENTS	TO DO
	7:00		TODAY'S PRIORITIES:
		A1 ❑ Schedule mtg. with Al	A1 ❑ Meeting with Big Al
	8:00	A2 ❑ Finish file for Adams	
			A2 ❑ ASAP file: Adams
	9:00	9–10 Sullivans; Client Meeting	
			A3 ❑ Urgent letter (Johnson)
	10:00		
		A3 ❑ Letter for Johnson	
	11:00		
	noon	11:30–1 Lunch/Seminar: Time Management	
	1:00	❑ Pick up HR forms	CALLS:
			❑ Dr. Ross appt.
	2:00	❑ Phone calls	❑ Order airline tickets
			❑ Change Wed. lunch
	3:00		
	4:00		
	5:00	❑ Pick up dry cleaning	
			AT HOME TO DO:
	6:00		❑ Pick up dry cleaning
	7:00		
	8:00		DISCUSS WITH SPOUSE:
			❑ Human resource forms
	9:00		

As we parted, I left Joanne with a list of time tips to simplify her day. This was just the beginning of good things to come her way.

Ten Time Tips to Simplify Your Day

1. Schedule the top ten things you need to do each day, and schedule them into the best time slots that will likely work for you.

2. Do self-initiated work early in the day like reports and writing projects before being pulled away to meetings, interruptions, and phone calls.

3. Create file folders with the following headings to keep your desktop clear and uncluttered:

> To Do
>
> To Call
>
> Projects
>
> Staff Meetings
>
> Personal

4. Assign tasks to a day and list them in your planner before putting files away for the day.

5. Schedule work on the hour and the half-hour to keep from getting distracted. Stay on track until the task is completed.

6. When you finish early, take a breather and complete an item that will take two minutes or less, like writing an e-mail, leaving a voice-mail message, or sending a fax.

7. Establish regular patterns for phone calls and stick to them, such as 8:30, 11:00, 2:00, and the end of the day.

8. Write out your afternoon work schedule before going to lunch. When you return, you'll know exactly what to do.

9. Keep a time log for three days and see where your time goes. (Use the 168-hours chart.)

> Total the hours and look for three things:
> - Three major time activities
> - Three big time wasters
> - Three tasks that aren't getting done

10. Delegate tasks to your support staff, such as sorting and prioritizing mail, setting appointments, returning phone calls when appropriate, keeping you on track according to your set schedule, and screening interruptions from outsiders.

Finding Time to Do Paperwork

The secret to finding time is studying your week and figuring out when you can make the most of your desk time. Try to develop a consistent schedule for working in your office, and make sure it is during the part of the day when you are the most alert.

When you keep your desk clear, you will get more accomplished in less time.

—LISA KANAREK, professional organizer

Simplify Your Desk

Simplify your work space to be the following:

- a pleasant place to get things done,
- a great place to make a difference,
- a space where you have everything you need to manage your work, your time, and your paper in an organized way.

A Fresh Start

Organizing your work space will be like having a fresh start at work—a new beginning. Your life will become easier because you've established a work space in which all of your paperwork and projects can be organized well and efficiently.

Disorganization causes fragmentation in thought and actions. Organization helps you accomplish tasks faster, which improves your reputation. The time you invest in organizing your work space will come back to you when you start saving time doing the work.

Whatever your situation, you can gain control of your paperwork and desk time at home and at work. Don't worry about your level of expertise; just do the next step. The most organized people constantly improve their systems to save time and get better results.

Personal Reflection

Where do you rate? To discover if you are getting the most out of your workday right now, ask yourself the following questions:

_____ 1. Do you find yourself often frustrated by the papers on your desk or in your files?

_____ 2. Is there regularly more than one pile of papers on your desk?

_____ 3. Do you think your paper problems would be solved if you had a different desk or set of file drawers?

_____ 4. Do you have a good reputation for following through on details?

_____ 5. Is there a clean work space in the center of your desk right now?

_____ 6. Do you regularly get your work done in a day?

_____ 7. Do you finish your day's work with peace of mind and a sense of accomplishment?

A Simple Prayer to Make a Difference

Dear God, thank You that You have a purpose for me in my job. Help me to recognize ways I can simplify my work space and time habits so I can better accomplish what is before me. Help me to make a difference in the world with the work I do today. Amen.

. . . .

Although it can be challenging to change ingrained behaviors, when you focus on all you have to gain, it's easier to succeed.

—JULIE MORGENSTERN, _Time Management from the Inside Out_

eleven

....

Simplify Your Parenting

Before becoming a mother, I had a hundred theories on how to bring up children. Now I have seven children and only one theory: love them, especially when they least deserve to be loved.

—KATE SAMPERI
A Special Collection in Praise of Mothers

Donna, a stay-at-home mom, was so excited about the systems she learned for managing her life that she wanted her three children to share in them as well. But she wasn't sure how to start. Her three children, ranging in age from four to twelve, had three very different personalities. Her oldest, Patrick, was in the seventh grade and very neat. Jonathan was a third grader who never had anything together. And four-year-old Tiffany loved to dance and sing so much that she hardly noticed anything amiss around her.

"There is so much out there about parenting styles, learning styles, and academic success," she said. "But I'd really like to have my children learn some life skills from a young age—like simplifying and organizing. I remember what I was like when I left home, and I'd like my children to be better prepared than I was. Is there anything I can teach them, especially since they are at different ages and stages?"

Step-by-Step Learning Sequence

Donna and other mothers like her found it helpful to know that there are specific skills that need to be taught at each stage of a child's development. The end goal is raising children who become capable young adults and leave home with a healthy self-esteem and the skills to manage life well.

We all want our children to grow up to be confident and self-reliant adults, but at this point we have to remember that we're still dealing with children. The lessons in organization need to be fun and rewarding. You will have greater success if you use a positive approach and model what you teach.

As parents we can help our children simplify their lives by dealing with several key areas pertaining to them:

- A family chore chart
- Cleaning up their bedroom
- Managing their papers
- Understanding age-appropriate tasks and rewards that lead to a simplified lifestyle

Family Job Chart

Donna and her family started with a family job chart, which I provided. It allowed her to teach her children to accomplish three easy jobs each day that were appropriate for their ages. Donna knew that consistency was important, so she needed to make a commitment to keep everyone's chores in mind.

Here is how Donna handled her family job chart:

- She listed only two to three jobs per day.

- She read the job chart after school and asked her children to complete two of the three jobs before dinner. The last job could be saved for after dinner.

- The total time for all three jobs would be only fifteen to twenty minutes, unless it was a specific homework lesson or music practice, which generally took longer. She outlined several sample jobs, such as setting the table, cleaning the table, unloading the dishwasher, putting laundry away, feeding the dog, cleaning the hamster cage, and dusting the tabletops.

- Finally, Donna said that Sunday was a day of rest—no jobs. They liked that!

Family Job Chart

	Patrick (7th grade)	Jonathan (3rd grade)	Tiffany (Preschool)
Monday	1. Practice trumpet 2. Do homework 3. Put laundry away	1. Do homework 2. Feed the dog 3. Unload dishwasher	1. Set table 2. Put away dress-up clothes 3. Take note next door
Tuesday	1. Practice trumpet 2. Do homework 3. Clean fish tank	1. Do homework 2. Feed the dog 3. Clean up toys in your room	1. Set table 2. Pick up toys in family room 3. Call Kim to play
Wednesday	(Follow same system through the rest of the week.)		
Thursday			
Friday			
Saturday			
Sunday	No Jobs!	No Jobs!	No Jobs!

One mother made the mistake of creating an elaborate poster board chart for her six children. In three short days, everything fell apart because it was too complicated and time-consuming for her to keep up. All you need is a white board or a simple computer-generated chart like the one above that can be reused week after week.

The Value of Chores and Job Charts

Karin, one of my clients, says she never had to do any chores as a child, so when she became an adult, she wasn't as disciplined or self-motivated as she wanted to be. Now a successful lawyer, Karin admits that it took a lot of work on her part to learn skills that she hadn't learned as a child.

"Motivation, discipline, and structure have become very important in life," she said. "I am still learning how to manage my time and my life because my parents did everything for me."

Learning how to start and finish a task, put away toys, and finish homework without constant reminders are big accomplishments for children—and opportunities for praise from parents. When you praise them in front of others, their self-esteem rises because they know they are important members of the family.

....

Children who contribute at home feel like valued members of the household. They take this attitude with them to the classroom, where they strive to be a productive member of that community as well.

—JAY DAVIDSON, *Teach Your Children Well*

....

Never Say, "Go Clean Your Room!"

A common mistake many parents make is issuing the time-honored command: "Go clean your room!" Telling a child to go clean his or her room is like telling an adult, "Go clean the basement before dinner!" The chore can seem overwhelming.

A better way to accomplish the same goal is to direct your child to one specific task, such as, "Please take a few minutes now and make your bed," "It's time to pick up your toys," or, "Before dinner, go put away the rest of your clothes." This teaches children to systematically approach pick-up before it becomes a major job. Keep in mind that for most children, and some parents, maintaining a clean bedroom is a big job.

Teaching children to deal with their rooms is like teaching them how to deal with life: There are easier ways to do things, and simplifying their approach to picking up their rooms is a rewarding part of life. After all, children's rooms are their whole world, and this should be the one place they can manage and enjoy.

Instead of ordering your children to clean their rooms, give them one easy chore to complete before the next meal. Whether they're six or sixteen, they will always appreciate your help. Join in and do some of the work with them to brighten their day if they are having a hard time. Help your children by having them follow these simple steps:

Five Steps to a Clean Bedroom

1. *Make the bed and make your day.* When the bed is made, 50 to 70 percent of the room is clean because the bed is often the largest surface. Make sure to have a comforter or an easy and attractive bedspread to pull up.
2. *Pick up everything from the floor and put it all away.* Start at the doorway and have them pick up everything on the floor. The floor makes a great play area, but it needs to be picked up before meals and bedtime.
3. *Clean the rest of the room by three categories: clothes, paper, and toys.*
   - Clothes: Put clean clothes away in drawers and dirty clothes in the hamper. Do this before bedtime so that you can start fresh the next day.
   - Paper and books: Organize all papers into notebooks, magazine holders, or colored files. Put books on bookshelves and give away ones they have outgrown.
   - Toys or favorite collections: The largest toys should be stored on the bottom shelves, and the ones with small pieces, like Legos or Barbies, should be kept up higher. Collections, however, can be displayed on dresser tops, with the front two-thirds of the dresser being kept clean.
4. *Add one extra cleaning area each week.*
   - Desktop: Keep new pencils and paper handy for school subjects and personal interests.
   - Nightstand: Make sure you have a good reading light to help children calm down at day's end.
   - Closet: Check each clothing item with your children to see if they want to keep or give away what's in their closet. Their sizes and tastes change often, so do this twice a year when you rotate summer and winter clothing.
5. *Empty the wastebasket often.* Keep a good-sized wastebasket handy and empty it often to minimize the clutter. Vacuum the floor at least once a week, too.

Create Special Memories Together

To complete your simplifying process with some extra touches, place a comfy chair in their room so that you can talk with them at night, or they can use it for reading during the day. Another thing you could do would be to paint their rooms and let them choose new posters or pictures for their walls. Let them become interior decorators for a day.

Spend some time together this weekend or next vacation simplifying your children's rooms. Look for opportunities to walk down the hall and say, "Katie, what a great job you did on your room!" After all, their room is their "world," and they will remember what you did together to make it a nice place to call home.

Handling the Kids' Papers

Many parents have a tough time knowing what to do with their children's papers. Just imagine how many papers they will accumulate from the time they enter preschool until they graduate from high school. We're talking several boxes! Here's an easy solution—the three-ring memory book.

A Memory Book That Works

- Buy a three-ring binder for each child, clear sheet protectors, and dividers. Put your child's most treasured papers and projects in clear sheet protectors in the binder.

- Label the spine with their name and the grade levels inside. Use dividers inside to separate the different school years.

- Create a cover of their grade-level school pictures. They will have fun watching themselves grow up chronologically on the memory book covers.

- Let the children add their choice of reading, spelling, writing, math, and science papers. They will choose what they are most proud of.

- Reduce poster-size projects at a place like Kinko's to fit into the sheet protectors.

- Take pictures of the children with their big projects and include the pictures in the memory book. In time, the child will be willing to toss the project and just keep the picture.

Don't worry if your children initially want to save every paper. After about second grade, it gets easier for them to part with papers from younger years. Remind yourself and your children, "The value is in doing the papers, not in saving all of them." The memory book is for saving representative memories of that phase of life. Updating the memory book at the end of each school year will ensure that school papers and reports are enjoyed, not stashed in the bottom of the closet.

Age-Appropriate Chores

Donna was especially excited when I shared the following chart. "This is what I've been looking for—a step-by-step plan of what to focus on with each child. I can see the progression laid out here," she continued. "Now I know what to do."

Like Donna, see what is listed for your children and then write the goals you want to focus on teaching them at that stage. Show them the chart and see what their reaction is. They may have missed some of the earlier skills, but they will understand that what you are asking is normal. A joint effort on both your parts will catch them up.

Age Level Growth Chart

AGE LEVEL	GOALS FOR YOUR CHILDREN	SKILLS FOR PROGRESSIVE INDEPENDENCE
Birth–1 yr.		• Fit into family sleeping habits • Play while parent cleans kitchen or does chores
Toddler 1–3 yr.		• Pick up toys in a small area (floor, shelf, table) and put away • Put books on shelves, clothes in hamper • Begin making choices between two items (outfits, drinks, activities)
Preschool/ kindergarten 3–5 yr.		• Dress self with help • Make bed daily with help • Carry belongings to and from car • Help set table and clear dishes • Practice good telephone habits with family members
Primary Grades (1–3)		• Make bed before breakfast or before school • Put away own things (backpack, lunchbox, coat) • Establish personal habits (wash hands, brush teeth, comb hair) • Empty dishwasher regularly • Write thank-you notes

AGE LEVEL	GOALS FOR YOUR CHILDREN	SKILLS FOR PROGRESSIVE INDEPENDENCE
Upper Grades (4–5)		• Put away clean laundry • Practice music or sports a regular number of times per week (may be started earlier if child shows interest) • Use charts or Post-it notes to remember things • Keep room neat • Clean out drawers and shelves
Middle School		• Be more self-reliant with homework and activities • Clean bathroom, closet, and drawers • Vacuum and dust • Do yard work and baby-sit • Make and buy gifts to give to family and friends
High School		• Do own laundry • Manage cash flow, banking, and vehicle expenses • Learn how to prepare three to five meals • Clean the kitchen after dinner • Shop for groceries and clothes • Prepare for moving on or to college

Your teens will be out on their own after high school, whether they're living in a college dorm room or in their own apartment. Whereas most dorm rooms are pretty messy and filled with mounds of dirty laundry, your college students can be among the amazing few who keep clean rooms and do their own wash. They'll be out on their own soon enough, so start teaching them now while they're still listening to you and watching you model your expectations.

Motivating Children to Action

Job + Timing + Motivation = Action

If your children or teens are not doing certain chores, it could be because

- the job is too big,
- the timing of the request is not realistic,
- the motivation is too small.

To get through these hurdles, you can try several things. Keep them company and do the task with them, or at least find something to do in the same room to keep them company. If you sense a lack of motivation, talk to them about their feelings. Perhaps something is bothering them, or perhaps they think they are doing more work than their brothers and sisters. Stay involved. And remember that your presence is the best motivator for children at any age.

Parents, it's our job to teach and train our children in the way they should go. When they finish their task or chore, check out how they did. They will appreciate the attention.

Children don't do what you expect, but only what you inspect.

—EMILIE BARNES, organization expert

Why Are Kids Inconsistent?

You may have a smoothly functioning family for several days only to discover that there are times that the family routine falls apart. What happens then?

Keep in mind where you are in the week. The weekends break the momentum of the weekly routine. Knowing this, plan Mondays to get back on track, reinforcing music, study, and bedtime habits to keep family life flowing. Children love routine as much as they love surprises. They just won't tell you so.

Tasks and Rewards

While there is definitely a place for family responsibility, a reward is also appropriate at times. Remember, it takes twenty-one times of practicing a new skill for it to become a habit.

Responsibility Formula Chart

No Task + No Reward = Dependency	Task + No Reward = Rebellion
No Task + Reward = Selfishness	Task + Reward = Responsibility

Isn't that a great chart? It's a wonderful reminder that the goal of chores is to instill a sense of responsibility and success in children, not just to have a clean house. The short-term goal of jobs is to get worthwhile chores done, while the long-term goal is to build a sense of responsibility.

When children are learning a new chore, like making a bed in elementary school years or washing clothes in the upper grades, it's wise parenting to attach a reward for a job well done. A youngster could get to play his favorite Nintendo game an extra fifteen minutes before bed or a teen could receive some extra gas money.

Laundry Builds Independence

One summer day my sixth-grade daughter, Christy, said to me, "Mom, you don't wash often enough!" I was rather defensive as I prided myself on being caught up, but I replied, "What is it you want? I just washed your clothes two days ago."

"My purple shirt," she said.

After a quick assessment of the situation, I led her to the washing machine. "I bet you can do your own wash," I said, "and I will pay you a dollar for every load." As we both realized what I had said, she lit up with glee, and I panicked that I would go broke. "But," I recovered, "you only get paid if you complete all four steps in the same day—wash, dry, fold, and put away."

That summer only cost me eight dollars before she said, "Mom, you don't have to pay me anymore. I like doing it myself." Two years later the same scenario was repeated with our second daughter, Lisa, as she became independent with her wash. Eventually our fourth-grade son, Mark, came to me and said, "Mom, I need some money." I sized him up to see if he could reach the washing machine and said, "Come here, have I got a deal for you!"

- -

Few things help an individual more than to place responsibility upon him and to let him know that you trust him.

—BOOKER T. WASHINGTON

- -

For teenagers, doing their own laundry also teaches them time-management skills. Want to wear a certain outfit tomorrow? Better get it into the wash today. Out of clean underwear? Do the wash immediately and plan better for next week. In a rush? Make a deal with your mom that if you get your laundry in the wash before school, she could help you out by drying, folding, and leaving it in your room so you could put it away after school.

The Key Is Consistency

The key to teaching children is consistency. Every Monday you need to reinforce the morning routine of making the bed, cleaning up the room, and doing chores before school. After school, greet them with a nutritious snack and hear about their day. Once they unwind, give them a choice of two chores they can do before dinner.

Keep bedtime at a regular time to give them a rested start on the next day. Keep the family dinnertime as consistent as possible, and the earlier in the evening the better. Children feel secure when the family routine is consistent.

Bringing Out the Best in Your Children

Your goal is to build systems that bring out the best in your children. The purpose of chores is to teach them independence and self-esteem. It is important to instill organization in your children, but to keep it in perspective. If the skills of organization are taught patiently and with love, eventually they'll take hold. It's more important to let your children know how much you love them, even when they forget to make their bed.

I am a firm believer that if you work orderly, you will think orderly. What a great help orderly habits at home can be for school and for a lifetime. Guide them in the way they should go, and don't give up.

Simplifying your parenting is all about knowing what's important to teach at each level—and teaching it consistently. Follow the chart, and someday your children will thank you.

Personal Reflection

1. What important organizational skills do I want my children to learn?

   _____

2. What does our family need to work on most when it comes to organizing space, time, or papers?

   _____

3. Which personal organizational skills do I need to improve to set a better example?

   _____

Training a child is about teaching, modeling, and coaching every day. I have found that training children is 50 percent by example and 50 percent by actually working on the child's skills.

Remember to teach your children that it's easier to live an organized life than a disorganized one. After all, don't we want to give our children the best foundation we can to succeed in life?

A Simple Prayer As a Mom

Dear God, thank You for my role as a mother. Please grant me the patience and wisdom I need to train my children as they grow up. When they're all grown up, what a blessing it would be to not only be their mom, but to be their friend—and have dinner at their house! Amen.

. . . .

She speaks with wisdom, and faithful instruction is on her tongue. . . .
Her children arise and call her blessed.

—Proverbs 31:26, 28

twelve

······································

Simplify the Holidays

The most important entertaining you will do this year, and especially during the Christmas season, will be in your own home with family.

—EMILIE BARNES
Christmas Is Coming

ince I became a professional organizer, my motto has been: "If you do anything more than once in life, organize it and simplify it." That means looking for ways to improve anything that you're sure you'll be doing again. When that happens, you'll feel more confident the next time you approach the situation, and better results are assured.

The holiday season definitely gives us an opportunity for improvement because it comes every November and December, right on schedule. I've long felt, however, that Thanksgiving and Christmas can bring us great joy, and with good planning, they won't be a big hassle at all.

My Story

While growing up, I should have watched more closely how the women in my family handled the holidays. Looking back, I can see how they were quite capable and actually quite impressive.

My mother was the queen of hosting overnight relatives, and I remember the time when we had twenty-five guests over the Christmas holidays. My twin aunts were always so far ahead of schedule that they leisurely enjoyed an annual holiday luncheon at the Marshall Field's department store while shoppers scurried around them. My mother-in-law was an outstanding cook and always had a delightful Norwegian smorgasbord ready for guests. And my sisters-in-law were to be envied for selecting and mailing their gifts before the post-office lines stretched outside the door. Each relative had a strength I admired, and they all handled the holidays so well.

I never placed myself in the same category as the other women in my family. I found myself struggling to decide what Christmas gifts to buy in mid-December, usually fighting the crowds with my children in tow. Living in Chicago at the time, it seemed that my shopping adventures coincided with icy roads and prevailing snowstorms.

I confess to staying up late on Christmas Eve wrapping presents and putting the final touches on my Christmas Day table settings. I don't even like to think about how I handled thank-you notes back then; with three children it was impossible to keep straight which presents came from whom.

I remember wondering, *Why can't I remember to start earlier each year? Isn't there an easier way to handle the holidays?*

Getting It Together

Personally, as I watched the capable women in my family, I realized they each had developed their own successful systems that took the stress out of the holidays. I, too, wanted to bring joy to other people and decided the holidays were as much a matter of organization as they were a matter of the heart. The two work together. Organization during the holidays is an expression of the heart.

And while I had the heart, it took me longer to find the systems. But I did, and you can, too! Let's look at several practical tools to simplify the most complex time of the year.

Christmas Came Early This Year

My turning point came when I stumbled onto a very valuable insight. Every year, one particular event occurs eight weeks before Christmas. Do you know what that is? It is Halloween. That event is important to note because you can use those eight weeks from

October 31 to December 25 as a structure to annually simplify and strategize your preparations.

Many people, myself included, have used Thanksgiving to trigger serious action steps for Christmas. It just didn't seem right to commercialize Christmas by purchasing gifts before Thanksgiving. But that's the problem. Waiting until after Thanksgiving does commercialize the holidays and puts us smack-dab in the middle of a mall with throngs of shoppers.

I also discovered that Thanksgiving is a "floating holiday." Some years it falls four and a half weeks before Christmas, and other years it comes as early as three and a half weeks. That is why you hear people say, "It seems like Christmas came early this year." Sometimes it does.

So check your calendar. If you are one of those people who relies on Thanksgiving to trigger your holiday energy, you should consider getting poised with your shopping list the day after Halloween—November 1.

Think of the Possibilities

Think of the possibilities if you kept all your holiday ideas in one place, divided up your tasks over eight weeks, and then followed your plan. You could be organized and less stressed for the holidays! This could be more of a reality if you would keep records from previous years and allow a time cushion for unexpected opportunities—or glitches.

Your Eight-Week Holiday Calendar

Notice the sample eight-week holiday calendar (on the following page) that can be used year after year. You can easily divide anything you need to do into this calendar.

Step 1: Fill in strategic dates to shape this year's structure, such as Halloween, November 1, Thanksgiving, Christmas Eve and Christmas Day, New Year's Eve and New Year's Day (which are exactly the same two days of the week as Christmas Eve and Christmas Day). If you celebrate Advent, mark those Sundays as well.

Step 2: Write in all the holiday celebrations you plan to participate in. Of course, you will receive invitations during the holiday season for various Christmas parties, but for now, write down events that seem to happen year after year. For instance, perhaps your church has the annual Christmas pageant the Sunday night before Christmas Day. Mark that down. Maybe your parents host the annual family Christmas Eve celebration. Write

Eight-Week Holiday Calendar

	Mon.	Tues.	Wed.	Thurs.	Fri.	Sat.	Sun.
8 Weeks Before:							
7 Weeks Before:							
6 Weeks Before:							
5 Weeks Before:							
4 Weeks Before:							
3 Weeks Before:							
2 Weeks Before:							
1 Week Before:							
Christmas Week!							
New Year's Week!							

that in. You might want to mark those events with a special symbol, such as a wreath or Christmas tree so they stand out as part of your seasonal celebrations.

Step 3: Highlight all the vacation days you will have with the kids or grandkids when they are home from school. Do you know your husband's work schedule? Does his office or factory shut down every year between Christmas and New Year's? Will you have any relatives staying with you? What about your own vacation plans?

Step 4: Number the weeks in the margin of your eight-week calendar and your monthly calendar like a countdown to Christmas week—3, 2, 1, and enjoy! Since most holiday get-togethers and events fall on weekends between Thanksgiving and Christmas, your chart will demonstrate the importance of doing your holiday shopping before Thanksgiving. Here's a sample schedule to accomplish your tasks in three phases over the eight weeks:

WHEN YOU HAVE OVERNIGHT GUESTS

Remember two key rules of successfully hosting family and guests during the holidays:

1. Keep them fed.
2. Keep them moving.

Phase 1: Gift Shopping and Wrapping

Eight weeks before: Shop and wrap one-third of your gifts.
Seven weeks before: Shop and wrap two-thirds of your gifts.
Six weeks before: Finish shopping and wrapping gifts.
Five weeks before: Start planning for Thanksgiving and vacation.

Phase 2: Decorations, Cards, and Mailings (between Thanksgiving and Christmas)

Four weeks before: Put up outdoor decorations and write Christmas cards.
Three weeks before: Set up the Christmas tree and decorate indoors. Mail gifts and cards.

Phase 3: Celebrations, Cooking, and Cleaning

Two weeks before: Attend and host parties. Bake and clean.
One week before: Grocery shop for Christmas meals and make final preparations for the big day.

Christmas Week: Celebrate Christmas and Enjoy!

You deserve a little down time, so take advantage of it.

New Year's Day

Take down decorations, write thank-you notes, and start the New Year fresh.

Organize Your Gift Giving

One of the biggest aspects relating to the holiday is gift giving. Create a Christmas list template to use from year to year. The more organized your records, the less trouble you will have thinking of new gifts to purchase.

Begin by making a chart with five columns and list the following:

- Each person you plan to get gifts for
- Ideas of what you want to give
- The dollar amount you plan to spend
- What you actually give
- What you spend

Check off the last column with a flourish in red pen when your gift is all wrapped and ready to give!

✓ COM-PLETED	NUMBER AND NAME	IDEAS	ACTUAL GIFT ($ Spent)	NEXT YEAR
	1. _____			
	2. Spouse			
	3. Child			
	4. Mom			
	5. Dad			
	6. Sibling			
	Etc			

Gift-Wrapping Center Solutions

Not only is it important to shop early, you need to wrap your gifts in a timely manner, as well. Creating a gift-wrapping center will solve many of those late-night wrapping dilemmas. Stock a storage box with all of the gift-wrapping supplies you need.

Simplify your holiday wrapping-paper selection to two or three color schemes and stretch it by having large-print, small-print, and solid-colored wrapping paper. Warehouse clubs often sell wrapping paper in bulk with these styles. Consistently choose either folded squares or rolled paper to simplify storage. Fresh white tissue paper perks up any gift or wrapping to make any box more special.

Complete your package wrapping with a matching bow for packages you hand-deliver and ribbons for packages that need to be mailed. Don't forget to purchase matching gift tags with room to write a sentence of warmth and love for the person you're giving it to.

Keep a special pen, scissors, and tape in the gift-wrapping center, and don't take those items to use elsewhere in the house. You don't want to be hunting for a pen and Scotch tape at the last minute.

> ### GIFT-WRAPPING CENTER
>
> Simplify your wrapping time with a gift-wrapping center in a storage box you can store under your bed or in a nearby closet. Be sure to coordinate the colors of the gift-wrapping items to minimize wrapping clutter.
>
> 1. Wrapping paper
> 2. Bows and ribbons
> 3. Tissue paper
> 4. Gift tags
> 5. Scotch tape
> 6. Scissors
> 7. A special marking pen
>
> The pen, scissors, and tape should never move from your gift-wrapping center.

Tips to Start Wrapping Early

To get yourself wrapping gifts early—before Thanksgiving—so that you can actually have time to enjoy the holidays, try these tips:

1. Turn on Christmas music to get yourself in the holiday mood for wrapping, even if it's an Indian summer day outside.
2. Time how long it takes to wrap a package and multiply that figure by the number of gifts. Then you'll have a rough estimate of how much time it's going to take.
3. Wrap and label your gifts within a day or two of purchasing them. Picture yourself waking up rested for Christmas Eve and Christmas Day.
4. Reward yourself when all your gifts are wrapped. Go out for coffee with a friend or shop for something for yourself. This can be a great motivator to get it all done!

Christmas Eve Surprise

Joan had always struggled with getting ready in time for Christmas, but she got excited about the idea of shopping early after I described it to her. She made some of her gifts in the fall, purchased others on sale, and ordered from catalogs before Halloween to simplify her shopping marathon. She told me that she was going to be prepared for this holiday season.

But when Christmas Eve arrived, she pulled her husband aside and whispered frantically, "Where are they?"

Looking confused he asked, "Where are what?"

"You know . . . the bags of Christmas toys that I bought last summer for the kids. I hid them in the garage, and now they aren't there!"

"I don't know," he said. "They weren't in those brown garbage bags that we sent off to Salvation Army last fall, were they?"

Suddenly the light dimmed in Joan's sparkling eyes.

A Holiday Notebook to Ease Stress

In that painful moment Joan learned the very reason to get organized for the holidays: You just can't remember everything. Even the best intentions can turn sour.

To avoid this scenario, create a holiday notebook to centralize all your lists and ideas. Find a simple but memorable (so you can find it) three-ring notebook, or you can use a section in your personal planner. Keep all your holiday organizing and plans in one place so everything is centralized and not floating around on scraps of paper. Keep your notebook next to your calendar at home and carry it with you when you go shopping. This will be a resource you can use year after year, too.

What should be in the holiday notebook?

- A list of people you plan to give presents to, what has been purchased, whether it is wrapped, and where it is stored (downstairs closet, under the stairway, or in what box in the garage). Don't forget that bags are temporary and often moved during the year while labeled boxes are more permanent.

- Eight-week calendars from past years with your comments about what worked and didn't work.

- Your holiday party menu and party plans. Include things you do annually so you don't have to start from scratch.

Fortunately for Joan, the stores were still open on Christmas Eve, so she hopped in her car for some last-second shopping. Joan chose not to let what happened ruin her Christmas. But on December 26, she purchased a lovely angel-blue notebook so that she could record all her hopes and dreams (and gift-hiding places) for the next year. She started making notes right away.

Christmas was meant to be enjoyed, and by planning ahead, it's easy!
—EMILIE BARNES, *Christmas Is Coming*

Final Steps for Simplifying Your Holidays

Three last areas must be looked at to see if they are complicating your holiday planning:

- Decorations
- Menus
- Meaningful traditions—or the lack of them

Simplifying Your Decorating

If your decorations cause you more anxiety than enjoyment, it is time to simplify. This is especially true if you seem to leave more of them packed away each year because you can't be bothered.

- As you come across pictures of good decorating arrangements in magazines, clip them out and keep them in your holiday notebook to simplify your decorating time next year.

- Simplify your decorations by getting them up early in December. What you don't put on display, give away to charity or a newlywed couple quickly so others can use them this year.

- Display decorations that bring you joy and warm your heart. This can be a creative manger scene, doll-like impressions of English carolers from the nineteenth century, or your favorite Christmas ornaments that mean something special to you. Decorating your home should be something you enjoy.

- When it comes time to decorate your tree, enlist the help of your children, or if they are too young, invite a girlfriend over to chat and hang ornaments with you. The task goes a lot faster with pleasant conversations.

- If you're looking for motivation, plan a neighborhood gathering or invite everyone from work to come over for your annual Christmas party. Opening up your home works as a good motivator to get everything in place!

- Simplify your boxes by labeling them clearly. Limit the amount of storage space they will absorb for the other eleven months of the year.

Decorating early in December will get you and your family ready and excited for the holidays. But when the holidays are over, they're over, so don't dally putting the decorations away.

Simplifying Your Menu Planning

The easiest way to simplify holiday meals is to write down what was well-received in the past in your holiday notebook. You can record what type of meats and side dishes were big hits with the family. Included here is a traditional dinner that will save you time and stress at Thanksgiving, Christmas, and New Year's.

The important thing is to be organized and give yourself every chance to succeed in the kitchen.

- You can purchase some of the basic ingredients for baking and cooking early in November so you don't strain the food budget in December. This is a particularly effective strategy if you see something on sale.

- Cut down the amount of time you spend baking by hosting or attending a cookie exchange with your friends.

- Jot down how long it takes to make your favorite krumkake or batches of holiday cookies so that you know if you'll have time to get everything baked when you have free time.

- Snap a picture of your family and friends enjoying their holiday meal. This pleasant memory will remind you how you decorated your table and what you served that evening.

Turkey Dinner Worksheet

Date/Occasion: Thanksgiving/Christmas   Time: eat at 5:00
Number of Guests: 8 adults, 3 teenagers

MENU	SERVING PIECE	GROCERY LIST
Turkey	good china platter	20 lb. turkey
		28 slices of white bread
Stuffing	oblong bowl	onion—1C, 1/2C
		celery—4C
Mashed Potatoes	big round bowl	eggs—3, 3
		poultry seasoning
Gravy	gravy boat	4 1/2 lb. potatoes
		butter—1/2 C
Green Beans	smaller round bowl	12 oz. cream cheese
		3/4 C sour cream
Orange Jell-O Salad	dinner plate	etc.
Jellied Cranberry	small sauce dish	Extras:
		soda milk
Rolls	basket	coffee
		coffee cream
Apple Pie	ceramic pie plate	napkins
		plastic wrap
Ice Cream	small dessert bowls	aluminum foil

COOKING TIMES	turkey 5–6 hours 325° oven	beans 10 min.
	potatoes 45 min. 350° oven	rolls 5 min.
TO DO TODAY:	make stuffing and put turkey in at 10:30 A.M.	
	potatoes in at 4:00 P.M.	make ice
	thaw rolls	dust
		clean bathroom

Favorite Holiday Traditions

One of my favorite holiday traditions happens between Christmas dinner and dessert. In our family, we lower the lights and take turns lighting an individual candle and sharing two blessings from the past year. This draws out the heart of the person in the warm glow of candlelight before dessert is served. When all the candles are lit, we sing "Joy to the World." At Thanksgiving you can use kernels of Indian corn to accomplish the same kind of reflection.

Another meaningful tradition is having the oldest (or youngest) family member read the Christmas story from Luke 2 before opening Christmas presents. To extend the special closeness as a family, continue reading a special devotional as a family by Christmas tree light during each night of vacation.

Celebrate the Reason for the Season

I wonder what would happen if we each put "Jesus" at the top of our Christmas gift list? You can, you know. Ask God to show you how to give back to Him. He might show you a down-and-out family in need of groceries, or prompt you to help out with the church Christmas pageant or give financially to worthy charities. When I give something of worth back to God, I find He multiplies that gift and organizes my time to get everything important done. That's because we have put Him first.

Countdown till Christmas

Perhaps you're reading this book during the holiday season and you're feeling overwhelmed because Christmas is just a week away. If that's the case, here's what you can do with the time you have left:

Five days before:
- Make out a remaining gift list and shop.
- Confirm any invitations and acceptances for Christmas dinner.

Four days before:
- Decorate and cleanup the house.
- Make a list of menus and a grocery list.

Three days before:
- Shop for groceries.
- Get laundry out of the way.

Two days before:
- Vacuum and clean up any piles.

One day before:
- Set the table.
- Run final errands.

Christmas Eve and Christmas Day:
- Set aside time to focus on the real meaning of Christmas.
- Keep ahead of the dishes and meals to keep things organized and peaceful.
- Enjoy the day and decide this will be the best Christmas ever!

STRESS-REDUCING TIPS FOR THE HOLIDAYS

1. Brighten up your calendar—and your outlook—with holiday stickers or a red pen marking holiday events.
2. Buy gifts in one major category this year—sweaters for everyone, appropriate CDs or books for mailed gifts, or personalized restaurant gift certificates.
3. Mark your calendar with two-hour appointments for Christmas preparations, such as Thursday, bake; Friday, decorate; Saturday, shop and clean.
4. Enlist a holiday buddy to help you plan, especially one who is better in an area you are weak in.
5. When you're doing the family Christmas cards, get an assembly line going. After you have addressed the envelopes, line up envelopes to stuff and stamps to lick.
6. Shop for convenience, whether it be online or at one mall to simplify the abundance of choices.
7. Call or e-mail the person that you just can't find that special gift for. Ask her what she would really like to get this year.
8. Stretch your limited social time by attending a Christmas event and getting together with friends for dinner beforehand or dessert afterward.
9. Purchase a holiday devotional book or novel to curl up with each night to get you through the season.
10. Savor one event or daily conversation by jotting it down in a Christmas journal. Title it "The Best Things That Happened to Me This Christmas."

Every holiday turns out different in some way—someone moves, someone marries, little children grow up, and older relatives have fewer years ahead of them than behind them. Whatever the situation, I'm confident you can simplify your plans and handle whatever comes.

Rediscover the joy of the season. Happy Thanksgiving, Merry Christmas, and Happy New Year to you and yours—one holiday at a time!

Personal Reflection

1. What do I like most about the holidays?

_____ Exchanging gifts with family and friends

_____ Decorating the house inside and out

_____ Sending Christmas cards and a family letter

_____ Contributing time or money to charities

_____ Attending special holiday events

_____ Baking cookies and specialty food

_____ Enjoying the extra time with family at home

_____ Spending the vacation doing something memorable

2. If I could only do one thing better this Christmas, I would really like to

_____.

3. If I could change one thing about the holidays, I would

_____.

4. One way to make this a great holiday for myself and others would be to

_____.

5. One new way I plan to honor God and celebrate the real reason for the season is by

_____.

A Simple Prayer for the Holidays

Dear God, You are the giver of all good gifts, so I ask for Your help with my plans to bless the people around me. Give me the vision and creativity to make this Christmas special. You understand . . . after all, You created the first Christmas. Amen.

. . . .

I bring you good news of great joy that will be for all the people. Today in the town of David a Savior has been born to you; he is Christ the Lord.

—LUKE 2:10–11

thirteen

....

Simplify Your Transitions

*What causes you to marvel? I marvel when I think back on my life's path
and see so clearly God's merciful intentions. Isn't hindsight perceptive?
Had I known back then what I know today, I would have relaxed more
in his care.*

—PATSY CLAIRMONT
The Women of Faith Daily Devotional

Every morning my husband, David, gets up at six o'clock with or without an alarm. Sixteen precise hours later, he goes to bed at 10 P.M. His pattern of transitioning in and out of his day is as predictable as a Fourth of July parade. Each morning, he anticipates a new beginning, and he moves smoothly from one event to another. He's an easy guy to live with, and I love how he even brings me a cup of tea on occasion. I know I can depend on him.

However, after years of marriage to such a dependable person, I am still about twenty minutes behind him. Oh, I'm always on time for events, but I don't keep the same orderly pace that he does. You see, I don't like to end things. I don't like to end the day and go to bed, I don't like to end my sleep and get up, and I don't even like to stop what I'm doing and leave the house.

That should have been my first clue as to how we would handle the transition of a major move across the country.

Can you guess who adjusted five minutes after getting off the airplane and who took five years to adjust? You're right—David was off and running as soon as we left the luggage carousel. As for me, I stewed about what happened to my life. That's when I began to look for a pattern about the unpredictable times women face—those planned and unplanned phases called transitions.

Just When You Think You Have Life under Control

Once you develop an organized and simplified lifestyle, you may feel that all is well and under control, but that may not be true. You are just in a good place at the moment. When things start to happen and you've been caught by surprise, however— a teenager in trouble, a sudden change in health, or losing a loved one—it's easy to feel like things are spinning out of control. That's when you enter a time of unexpected transition.

Other times we have transitions that we anticipate, like getting married, having a baby, moving to a new house, or retiring after a lifetime of hard work. But knowing it is coming doesn't make it any easier.

A transition can happen by choice or by chance. It doesn't really matter how it happens—it matters how you handle it. How you handle a transition determines the mark it leaves on your life. It can either blend into the passages of time or leave a scar reminding you of the pain.

In this chapter, we'll look at four situations: moving, health changes, losing a loved one, and weddings. We'll look at ways we can handle these transitions with more finesse and less stress.

Transition Patterns

After several painful transitional times of my own, I learned that transitions don't always have a clean start and a tidy ending. Webster's dictionary defines *transition* as "the passing from one activity, place, or condition to another."

William Bridges, author of the book *Transitions,* writes that transitions have three natural phases:

1. *An ending.* This signals that something is over, and we need to let go of the people and places who once defined who we were.

2. *The neutral zone.* This temporary time between an ending and a new beginning is an important phase to reorient your life and direction.
3. *The new beginning.* This is the time when you are physically and emotionally ready to move into a new phase.

The first and last phases are pretty obvious, but sometimes we encounter a rocky neutral zone in the middle without knowing why. That's what happened to me, as you'll soon see.

Simplify the Transition: Moving

Our recent phase of family transitions began with a cross-country move from Rochester, New York, to San Diego, California, for my husband's work. I was leaving behind thirteen years of raising our children from preschool through high school, a home church with fulfilling ministries, and my flourishing speaking and consulting career.

David's new job started so rapidly that we didn't even have time to find a home to move into. The company settled us into a Marriott Residence Inn for what turned out to be eight long, interminable weeks. I woke up each morning to the same questions: *Where am I? How did I get here? What am I to do today?*

That's when I called Kathy, a wise counselor and my friend from back home. "Kathy," I asked, "what in the world do I do when I have no responsibilities and very little to do? You know I am a doer and someone who needs a place to call home."

"There's one thing you can be doing when you are in transition. When you can't control the external, focus on the internal," Kathy said.

....

A life lesson for when you are in transition: When you can't control the external, focus on the internal.

—KATHLEEN ELLIOTT, executive director of Agape Counseling Associates

....

Her advice helped me relax. I started doing some reading and looking at the temporary housing time as a vacation. After all, when you move three thousand miles to a new city where you don't know anybody and nobody knows you, there aren't a lot of distractions.

I focused on spending time with the five of us and discovering our new hometown. Eventually we moved into a new home, and life began settling into a routine.

Our move actually bonded us as a family. After all, we only had ourselves those first few months until we made friends and settled in. Our children were amazed by the Southern California lifestyle, where they could take surfing as a P.E. class or walk outside to change classrooms. High schoolers just didn't do that in New York, but you could in California. We looked at everything as a West Coast adventure, but at the same time, I have to confess that I stayed in the neutral zone of the transition for a long time, and I didn't know why.

Three-Part Transition: Moving

PERSON IN TRANSITION	1. AN ENDING	2. THE NEUTRAL ZONE	3. THE NEW BEGINNING
• Mom (that would be me)	• Move from New York to California	• Temporary housing • Parenting teens through the transition • Looking for new roles	• Making friends, finding a church • Joining several new groups

STEPS TO SIMPLIFY YOUR MOVING

1. Take pictures to preserve good memories. Take lots of pictures of your old home and friends.
2. Start a moving notebook. Keep lists in it such as

   • Hopes and Dreams for My New Home
   • Things to Remember to Do
   • Things to Sell or Give Away

3. Downscale room by room. Start by emptying rooms that won't be in your new home (for example, an extra bedroom and closet or a basement).
4. Give yourself permission to leave bad memories behind. Whether it's an old sofa or a garage full of clutter, leave it behind. The bigger, the better!

5. Take your favorite things that bring you pleasure. Choose one box of things that make you smile and unpack it early.
6. Use one room for "get rid of" stuff and empty it often. Plan garage sales and organize pick-ups from charities early on.
7. Maintain order in your regular living areas. Don't create piles for the move in the family room and kitchen.
8. Accept the offers of friends. Accept offers to bring meals and help you pack. Cherish the extra time together.
9. Don't pay to move anything you don't love! When you unpack, you will be surrounded by "good" stuff you like.
10. Use garage sale income for your new home. Buy new towels or something pretty to help the transition.

Simplify the Transition: Health

A year after we moved to San Diego, we said good-bye to our oldest child, Christy, as she traveled cross-country to college in Chicago—another transition for David and me.

Around Valentine's Day, our second daughter, Lisa, was feeling run down and tired in high school. David and I had longstanding plans to go away on a weekend cruise, so we took her in for a checkup. After examining her, the doctor reassured us. "Just keep her home and resting," he said. We reluctantly left her in the care of a neighbor for the weekend.

When we arrived home, we learned that Lisa had been hospitalized the night before for severe flulike symptoms. The doctors performed a spinal tap, at which point her health collapsed. Lisa never returned to school to complete her junior year. We were stunned.

This transition was definitely unexpected. Lisa and I spent days, weeks, and months going to specialists to ease her pain. Each week we hoped that by "next Monday" she would be back in high school. That never happened.

I still remember the nights my husband carried Lisa up the stairs to bed because of numbness and pain. His steadiness and her courage gave me strength. And old friends and new friends prayed for her healing.

Other good folks helped us through the long neutral zone of this health transition, like the little five-year-old girl who asked her daddy, one of Lisa's teachers, if he would deliver a gift of pink nail polish to my daughter. When he asked her why, the kindergartner innocently replied, "Because when she looks down at her pretty nails, then she can feel happy."

Lisa's illness turned out to be full-blown mononucleosis with severe migraines. The disease ravaged her for three months straight. The migraines finally subsided, but the mono took longer. Just when we thought things were getting better, the rheumatologist exclaimed, "Oh, my goodness, Lisa has fibromyalgia!" Our hearts sank as we realized Lisa now had a lifelong painful condition. She was at risk for even finishing high school.

Six months into the ordeal, we received a phone call from a doctor in South Dakota who was able to help Lisa. His treatment plan started to relieve the pain and fatigue. She began to improve slowly but steadily. We saw glimmers of hope.

In September of her senior year, Lisa made it to school more days than she missed. In time she gave up her handicapped-parking sticker, and with great determination she graduated with honors with her high-school class!

She made it through her health transition over the next four years and recently graduated from college. Lisa is back to life—a different life—but still as a beautiful, talented girl with a wiser and more tender heart. We thank God for giving her a second chance at life.

. . . .

When you think things cannot get any worse, God carries you farther into the valley and comes out holding your hand.

—LISA RAMSLAND, her high-school yearbook quote

. . . .

Three-Part Transition: Health

PERSON IN TRANSITION	1. AN ENDING	2. THE NEUTRAL ZONE	3. THE NEW BEGINNING
• Lisa	• Healthy high-school girl becomes ill	• Long illness and diagnosis during high school	• Day by day
• Mom (me)	• Suddenly the mother of a very sick teenager	• One year recovering, three years to stabilize	• Seeing Lisa go to college and function on her own

HEALTH TO ILLNESS TRANSITION TIPS

For the patient:

1. Focus on little improvements you see and not on where you used to be.
2. Fill your mind with truth and the most positive outlook you can muster.
3. Accept the help of people around you, and be grateful for each day you make it through the pain and medical tests.
4. Celebrate anything you can.
5. Accept that people will not know what to say or how to help you, but appreciate their good intentions.
6. Gravitate to those who are a source of strength.

To the caregiver:

1. Be the advocate for your patient to move him or her forward to better health.
2. Keep yourself strong and healthy so you will be able to pour your energies into his or her recovery.
3. Remember you are a source of strength, so deal with your emotions with other friends, not your patient.
4. Give him or her hope. When your patient has none, he or she will cling to yours.

Simplify the Transition: Loss

I had companionship throughout Lisa's health crisis—my mother-in-law, Nana, who was taking care of my father-in-law after he started displaying symptoms of Alzheimer's. As serious as both situations were, we could still support one another and laugh about how our "patients" did for the day.

Like the times Poppy put his clothes on backward, or stole ice cream in the night and put the soggy box back into the refrigerator instead of the freezer. When he developed liver cancer, however, we knew the end was coming. We prepared ourselves for another transition.

On the same day Poppy peacefully died in his sleep under hospice care, a jarring piece of news came our way. My dear Aunt Lor, who had supported me with love and regular phone calls over the years, fell and apparently had a stroke. At eighty-five years young, she had never been sick in her life. My source of strength here on earth was crushed.

That was the darkest day of my life: my daughter was barely functioning, my father-in-law had died, and my dear aunt had a stroke. I cried out to God that day, "How much more can one person take?" as I dissolved into tears.

Everything works out right in the end.
If things are not working right, it isn't the end yet.
Don't let it bother you, relax and keep on going.

—Michael C. Muhammad

Strength for the Day

The good thing is that when you hit bottom, God gives you strength for the day and the only way out is moving forward. For us at that time that meant attending Poppy's funeral in Chicago. Three weeks later, we flew across the continent to Florida, this time to visit Aunt Lor at her lowest point. The trip was difficult because Lisa had to be wheeled through several airports, but Lisa really wanted to see her great-aunt who had been her support in crisis.

I thought back to a conversation a couple months earlier when my daughter called Aunt Lor. "So what have you been doing lately?" Lisa asked.

"I haven't done anything, Lisa, because I've been praying for you all day," she replied.

My daughter was blown away. People like Aunt Lor are the ones you want to know when you go through painful transitions. They carry you in their hearts.

Sadly Aunt Lor passed away six weeks after Poppy. Life wasn't getting any easier, but we were getting stronger as we moved through each transition. There must be better times ahead, we reasoned.

Fear comes from feeling out of control. Hope comes from knowing who is in control. And hope comes from knowing that we have a sovereign, loving God who is in control of every event of our lives.

—Lisa Beamer, *Women of Faith* magazine

Are You Okay?

One transition prepares us for the next. About a year later my own father was in hospice care and I was more aware of what would be happening and how I would handle it. In time, he passed away peacefully, and I was proud of his years of perseverance through the pain of arthritis.

For the next few hours after the news, I felt a sense of heightened alertness. Now that the news was final, I kept checking in with myself, and I really thought I was okay. I needed to run an errand. But as I drove along, I glanced up and realized I had just run a red light and driven straight through an intersection. *Wow, I'm not okay,* I thought. *I need to get home.*

Even though you know it's coming, the news still hits you hard. Losing a parent is like losing a piece of your security. Never minimize the impact it will have on you.

A Second Life Lesson

During times of loss, don't trust yourself to be functioning normally for some time. Rely on the help of those around you until you get your bearings again.

Three-Part Transition: Loss

PERSON IN TRANSITION	1. AN ENDING	2. THE NEUTRAL ZONE	3. THE NEW BEGINNING
• Mom (me)	• Deaths of father-in-law, dear Aunt Lor, then my father	• Dealing with losing relatives • Lisa improving	• Accepting losses • Receiving support of relatives

Simplify the Transition: Better Times Ahead

It's important to peacefully close painful chapters in our lives because better ones are often waiting ahead. In our family, life's pain subsided as we experienced the wedding of our oldest daughter. It was the cycle of life: There is loss in death, but there is renewal in weddings and new babies that will surely come into the world.

When our oldest daughter, Christy, became engaged seven months after my father's funeral, we were ready for a season of happiness. What a good experience for the family to gather together on such a joyous occasion. A nephew's wedding three months later re-confirmed that there is happiness in life after hard times. Look for them. You can expect them.

Advice to Brides (and Families) about Weddings

1. Enjoy the time from engagement to the wedding. It is a fun time because everyone loves a love story.
2. Spend equal time planning your marriage as you do planning your wedding day. It sets the stage for a good life together.
3. Enjoy the decisions of where to live, what you'll do as a new bride, and how to set up a home as a chance to get to know your spouse and make decisions together.
4. Shift your loyalties from your family to your spouse. Put him first.
5. Organize and pare down your stuff before you move into your new home.
6. Start to combine your calendars and schedules during your engagement. Think in terms of "we" on your calendar, not just "me."

Three-Part Transition: Wedding

PERSON IN TRANSITION	1. AN ENDING	2. THE NEUTRAL ZONE	3. THE NEW BEGINNING
• Mother (me)	• Daughter getting married	• Engagement and wedding planning	• Seeing newlyweds' apartment and knowing they are happy

Change Points Create a New You

Having gone through all the transitional times and coming out the other end, I can attest to the need to make sense of losses and transitions.

Often you can get flashes of insight that give everything a new perspective. For me, it was a story described by Dr. Charles Stanley in his book *The Blessings of Brokenness* that put my life into perspective.

It seems that one day a woman approached Dr. Stanley, a famed pastor from Atlanta, and told him that it felt like years since God had used her. "Does God still have something for me?" she asked.

The pastor questioned her, asking when was the last time she ever felt like God was trying to change something in her life. She couldn't think of a time. So Dr. Stanley asked, "Have you ever had any great problems in your life—difficulties that seemed to pull the rug out from under your feet emotionally, spiritually, perhaps even physically?"

"Oh, yes," she said, "but I just waited them out."

"Did those problems change anything in you?"

"No," she said with great resolution. "I'm a survivor. I didn't change a bit. I stuck to my guns."

"That's likely the problem," said Dr. Stanley. "As long as you refuse to recognize the ways in which the Lord desires for you to grow and change, the Lord can't trust you to do His bidding. . . . He has a great and wonderful purpose and plan for your life, but He can't bring you into the fullness of it as long as you refuse to grow and change in your spirit."

After reading that story, the pieces of my life fell into place: My purpose was to grow and to change through each transition. No longer was my goal in trials to simply survive—it was to grow into more maturity, to be transformed into tenderness of heart, and to develop strength of character.

The hard times in my life all started to make sense. I was going to be fine. And so are you!

. . . .

However you have learned to deal with them, endings are the first phase of transition. The second phase is a time of lostness and emptiness before life resumes an intelligible pattern and direction, while the third phase is that of beginning anew.

—WILLIAM BRIDGES, *Transitions*

. . . .

Personal Reflection

To help you through a particularly hard time that you can't make sense out of, try journaling the answers to these questions. It will help you "emotionally relocate" and let your emotions catch up to what is happening around you. You really can make it through every transition you face. God will not give you more than you can handle with His help.

Steps to Make Sense of Your Transition

1. Name the transition: _____

2. What was I like before this transition?

_____

3. How have I grown because of this experience?

_____

3. What did I do well (or am doing well) through this transition?

_____

4. Are there people I need to thank for helping me through this transition?

_____

5. What got me through the transition?

_____

6. Is there anything I have to resolve before I can move forward?

_____

7. Is there any way this transition can be used in a positive direction?

_____

A Simple Prayer of Faith

Dear God, sometimes transitions are hard for me. Would You put Your tender loving arms around me and hold me when I'm afraid, and fill me with courage and vision when I need to take action? I thank You for family and friends. I pray for strength for the day, and I cling to the promise that You will always be with me. Amen.

. . . .

[She] will have no fear of bad news;
[her] heart is steadfast, trusting in the LORD.
[Her] heart is secure, [she] will have no fear;
in the end [she] will look in triumph on [her] foes.

—PSALM 112:7–8

Conclusion

Simply put—you can do this.
You're ready.
Just keep at it!

fourteen

· ·

Simply Put—You Can Do This!

To enjoy life to the full, keep it simple.

—JOYCE MEYER
Celebration of Simplicity

*A*fter our long season of transitions, things got back to normal and we celebrated the happy occasion of our first child, Christy, getting married. The way I saw it, a wedding was a great opportunity to leverage getting something extra done around the house. "Honey," I said to my husband, David, "don't you think we could do something special—like getting the house painted? We could really use a paint job outside anyway, and all these people are coming."

After many discussions and a half-dozen paint bids, the process finally began. The house was power-washed, the trim was scraped, and the outside walls were patched. Finally, our home was painted, and the house took on a new glow. It looked great!

But do you know what was even better? The windows got so dirty in the process that they had to be cleaned. They sparkled in the sunlight so much that the sky actually looked bluer, and the grass certainly looked greener.

That's what it is like to organize and simplify your life. You take the time to organize one thing, and two great things happen—the project gets done and your outlook on life gets brighter. You just feel better on both accounts.

That same feeling can happen every day. When you set up your personal organizing center, you can routinely process the mail and clear the counter. When you know what's for dinner, you can handle any delays that crop up late in the day. When you have a good game plan to accomplish your projects, you will feel secure that things will be completed. Life just looks better and works better when you persist in simplifying everyday living.

One of my organizing classes listed all the benefits of getting organized and simplifying life. Simplifying life means you

- save time,
- don't have to look for things,
- think clearer,
- are a nicer person,
- feel better about yourself,
- save money,
- have less stress,
- are more productive,
- don't feel guilty,
- have more time for people,
- don't feel embarrassed.

Simplifying your life means organizing your time, your home, your office, and special seasons so they work for you, not against you. Take the time to work through the PuSH System from the project stage of setting it up right, to a system that is easy to maintain, and finally to a habit that becomes so natural you always keep it simple and organized.

And now that you know what to do, I know you can do it. You will experience a sense of freedom and order when everything is as it should be. The goal in organizing your life is not to be perfect, but to get better. Keep taking steps every day in that direction.

When God created us, He gave us the gift of time. He knows the number of our days, and although we don't, the Bible talks about planning those days wisely. If we live until we're eighty years old, we will have 29,200 days to start fresh each morning. That's a lot of days. With all that opportunity, we can reshape our lives by reshaping our days.

We have covered a lot of ground in this book, and I congratulate you for reading through to the end. You are a precious, wonderful woman with an important role in life that only you can fill. Make every day count for you and for the people around you.

You're ready. You're well equipped to handle anything that comes your way, and I'm thrilled that you've made the effort to change your life.

I believe you can simplify your life—for good! Just keep at it, and even you will be amazed at the results.

Warmly,
Marcia Ramsland
Professional Organizer

A Simple Prayer for Change

Dear God, I believe You have a purpose for me, and that means accomplishing things in life. Forgive me for thinking undone things are more spiritual because I am waiting for some divine inspiration rather than taking action. May my closet cleaning, my new time schedule, and my clutter pick-ups make You smile as I look intently into Your heart and to my circumstances to figure out Your will for me. I know this is a new beginning in my life. Help me to follow through on my plans and dreams. Amen.

. . . .

I firmly believe we can do what we set our mind to. It takes time and commitment and faith, but God is in the business of miracles. Don't give up. You have no idea what's ahead for you.

—Luci Swindoll, *The Women of Faith Daily Devotional*

About the Author

Marcia Ramsland is a professional speaker and organizer whose passion is to help people live life well. She helps clients and audience participants conquer organization problems to simplify their lives and lifestyles. She is the president of Life Management Skills. She and her husband live in San Diego, and they are the parents of three adult children.

To contact Marcia for speaking engagements, personal consulting, or sharing how this book has touched your life, write

Marcia Ramsland, President
c/o Life Management Skills
P.O. Box 721792
San Diego, CA 92172

e-mail: Simplify@OrganizingPro.com
www.OrganizingPro.com

Acknowledgments

*A*ny project of this size means that a team of people surrounded the author. For this reason I would like to thank some very special people who helped me accomplish this goal.

The highest appreciation goes to my family: my dear husband, David, and our three grown children, Christy, Lisa, and Mark. They allowed me to share my passion for organizing and speaking during their growing-up years and continue to support me today.

Special thanks immediately goes to Debbie Wickwire and Mark Sweeney at Thomas Nelson, and Mary Graham and the Women of Faith team who believed in me and my message. I love you all.

Lee Hough, Linda Glasford, and Chip MacGregor at Alive Communications walked me through the literary process, as did author and novelist Randy Ingermanson. Mike Yorkey edited and reworked my manuscript sentence by sentence, for which I am most grateful.

Several professional groups of friends also deserve recognition including my team members of the You Can! Conference Speaking Team, the San Diego Christian Writer's

Guild, Karen O'Connor's critique group, my Prayer Team, and CLASS Reunion with Florence and Marita Littauer. Their camaraderie and guidance were invaluable.

Special thanks goes to Heather Reider and her sister, Paige Jennings, who originally encouraged me to write this book. And to my mentors, Dr. Denis Waitley and Pam Farrel, who spoke encouraging words just when I needed them.

Another group of people supporting this project are my professional organizing colleagues whom I met years ago. Today we continue a joint quest to make the world a better place through organization, including Julie Morgenstern, Barbara Hemphill, Ruth Wong, Harold Taylor, Ann Gambrell, Paulette Ensign, Alexis Joseph, the San Diego chapter, and the National Association of Professional Organizers (NAPO).

Finally, the biggest thanks goes to God, who gives me eyes to see wonderful things in life each day; to my Mom, who taught me to pay attention to routine systems going on around me; and to my Dad, who would have been so proud of me.

Resources

Time Management

Finding More Time in Your Life, Dru Scott Decker (Harvest House, 2001)

The Idiot's Guide to Overcoming Procrastination, Michelle Tullier (Alpha Books, 1999)

Making Time Work for You, Harold Taylor (Harold Taylor Time Consultants, 1998)

Seven Habits of Highly Effective People, Stephen Covey (Simon & Schuster, 1990)

Time Management from the Inside Out, Julie Morgenstern (Henry Holt and Company, 2000)

You Can Find More Time for Yourself Every Day, Stephanie Culp (Betterway Books, 1994)

Office and Paper Management

Home Office Life: Making a Space to Work at Home, Lisa Kanarek (Rockport Publishers, 2001)

Organized to Be Your Best! Susan Silver (Adams Hall Publishing, 2000)

Simplify Your Worklife, Elaine St. James (Hyperion, 2001)

Taming the Paper Tiger at Work, Barbara Hemphill (Kiplinger, 2002)

Life Management

The Gentle Ways of the Beautiful Woman, Anne Ortlund (Inspirational Press, 1998)

Life Management for Busy Women, Elizabeth George (Harvest House, 2002)

Organizing from the Inside Out, Julie Morgenstern (Henry Holt and Company, 1998)

The Path: Creating Your Mission Statement for Work and for Life, Laurie Beth Jones (Hyperion, 1998)

Women Who Do Too Much, Patricia Sprinkle (Zondervan, 2002)

Home and Family

Clutter's Last Stand, Don Aslett (Writer's Digest Books, 1984)

The Family Manager Takes Charge, Kathy Peel (Perigee, 2003)

How to Get Kids to Eat Great and Love It, Christine Wood, M.D. (KidsEatGreat, Inc., 1999)

More Hours in My Day, Emilie Barnes (Harvest House, 2002)

The New Messies Manual, Sandra Felton (Fleming H. Revell Company, 2000)

Open Heart, Open Home, Karen Mains (InterVarsity Press, 2002)

Teach Your Children Well, Jay Davidson (Tojabrel Press, 2000)

The Treasure inside Your Child, Pam Farrel (Harvest House, 2001)

Life Transitions

After the Boxes, Susan Miller (Focus on the Family, 1995)

The Blessings of Brokenness, Charles Stanley (Zondervan Publishing House, 1997)

Let's Roll: Ordinary People, Extraordinary Courage, Lisa Beamer (Tyndale, 2002)

Transitions, William Bridges (Perseus Books, 1980)

Additional Quoted Books

Celebration of Simplicity, Joyce Meyers (HarperCollins, 1999)

Christmas Is Coming, Emilie Barnes (Harvest House, 1998)

Living the Simple Life: A Little Treasury, Elaine St. James (Andrews McMeel Publishing, 2000)

Talking So People Will Listen, Florence and Marita Littauer (Servant Publications, 1998)

A Woman God Can Use, Pam Farrel (Harvest House, 1999)

The Women of Faith Daily Devotional (Zondervan, 2002)

Web Sites:

Day Runner—www.dayrunner.com

Day-Timer—www.daytimer.com

Kinkos—www.kinkos.com

National Association of Professional Organizers—www.napo.net

Office Depot—www.officedepot.com

Office Max—www.officemax.com

Staples—www.staples.com

Women of Faith—www.womenoffaith.com

Reference Terms

This list of organizing terms is original to the author unless they are common identifications. Practice these systems daily to simplify your life.

WOMEN OF FAITH®
LIFE STYLE

Women of Faith's LifeStyle products offer practical resources designed to connect with and encourage women in everyday life. Focusing on realistic needs and current trends, each product selected fulfills the Women of Faith mission of nurturing women spiritually, emotionally, and relationally. Topics addressed include organization, decorating, entertaining, finance, and health.

WOMEN OF FAITH MISSION STATEMENT

Women of Faith wants all women to know God loves them unconditionally, no matter what. The ministry reaches out through motivational, yet moving conferences. Since 1996, more than 3,000,000 women have attended Women of Faith events in dozens of cities across North America.

Women of Faith is a nondenominational women's ministry committed to helping women of all faiths, backgrounds, age groups, and nationalities be set free to a lifestyle of God's grace. Founded specifically to meet the needs of women, Women of Faith is committed to nurturing women spiritually, emotionally, and relationally—whether it be in marriages, friendships, the workplace, or with their children. Our goal is to provide hope and encouragement in all areas of life, especially those that can wear women down and steal their joy and hope.

Women of Faith, which has become America's largest women's conference, exists to deliver great news to women: God loves them, and there are a bunch of girlfriends out there who love them too! Through laughter, music, dramas, and gut-level, real-life stories about how God has worked through the good and bad of our lives. Women of Faith reminds women that God is crazy about them!

For more information or to register for a conference, please visit *womenoffaith.com*